BEHOLD

Study Outlines of the Book of REVELATION

RANDY WHITE

Copyright © 2017 Randy White
Cover and Illustration: Leonardo Costa
Cover and Illustrations © 2017 DispensationalPublishing House, Inc.

All rights reserved. This book or any portion thereof may not be reproduced or used in any manner whatsoever without the express written permission of the publisher except for the use of brief quotations in a book review.

Scriptures quoted as KJV are taken from the KING JAMES VERSION (KJV).

Printed in the United States of America
First Edition, First Printing, 2017
ISBN: 978-1-945774-12-6

Dispensational Publishing House, Inc.
220 Paseo del Pueblo Norte
Taos, NM 87571

www.dispensationalpublishing.com

Ordering Information: Quantity sales. Special discounts are available on quantity purchases by churches, associations, and others. For details, contact the publisher at the address above.

Orders by U.S. trade bookstores and wholesalers. Please contact the publisher:
Tel: (844) 321-4202

1 2 3 4 5 6 7 8 9 10

Dedicated to the faithful group of believers from around the world who have joined me on Thursday nights for online Bible study for nearly seven years. Their eager anticipation of digging into the Word has made me a more diligent teacher. Though we are separated by miles, we gather as brothers and sisters, as if we were around a small table, and open the Word together.

Table of Contents

PREFACE 11

INTRODUCTION OF THE REVELATION 13
    Revelation 1:1a: *The Content of the Revelation* *13*
    Revelation 1:1b-2: *The Source of the Revelation* *14*
    Revelation 1:3: *The Blessing of the Revelation* *14*

  Revelation 1:4-7: *The Greeting* *15*
    Revelation 1:4: *The Penman and the Recipients* *15*
    Revelation 1:4b-5a: *The Author* *15*
    Revelation 1:5b-7: *The Doxology* *16*

  Revelation 1:8 : *The Declaration of God the Father* *17*

  Revelation 1:9-11: *The Context and the Instruction* *17*
    Revelation 1:9: *From Whom, Where, and Why* *17*
    Revelation 1:10a: *John, Taken Away and Hearing a Voice* *18*
    Revelation 1:10b-11: *The Instruction* *19*

  Revelation 1:12-16: *The Sight John Beheld* *20*
    The Fourfold Sight 20
    The Description of the Savior 21

  Revelation 1:17-20: *The Comfort and Instruction to John* *22*
    Revelation 1:17: *Jesus as the First and the Last* *22*
    Revelation 1:18: *Jesus as Ruler of Life* *23*
    Revelation 1:19-20: *The Instruction to Write and a Mystery Revealed* ... *23*

REVELATION 2-3: *THE LETTERS TO*
THE SEVEN CHURCHES 25
  Interpretations of the Seven Churches 25
    The Historical Interpretation 25
    The Prophetic Interpretation 26
    The Futurist Interpretation 27
    Who Are the "Angels" of the Churches? 28

  Revelation 2:1-7: *The Church at Ephesus* *28*
    Revelation 2:1: *The Description of Christ* *28*
    Revelation 2:2-6: *The Message to the Messenger* *28*

    Revelation 2:7: *The Message to the Church* *30*
Revelation 2:8-11: *The Church at Smyrna* *30*
    Revelation 2:8: *The Description of Christ* *30*
    Revelation 2:9-11: *The Message to the Messenger* *31*
    Revelation 2:10-11: *The Message to the Church* *32*
Revelation 2:12-17: *The Church at Pergamos* *32*
    Revelation 2:12: *The Description of Christ* *32*
    Revelation 2:13-16: *The Message to the Messenger* *33*
    Revelation 2:17: *The Message to the Church* *34*
Revelation 2:18-29: *The Church at Thyatira* *34*
    Revelation 2:18: *The Description of Christ* *34*
    Revelation 2:19-23a: *The Message to the Messenger* *34*
    Revelation 2:23b-29: *The Message to the Church* *36*
Revelation 3:1-6: *The Church at Sardis* *36*
    Revelation 3:1: *The Description of Christ* *36*
    Revelation 3:1-4: *The Message to the Messenger* *37*
    Revelation 3:5-6: *The Message to the Church* *37*
Revelation 3:7-13: *The Church at Philadelphia* *38*
    Revelation 3:7: *The Description of Christ* *38*
    Revelation 3:8-11: *The Message to the Messenger* *38*
    Revelation 3:12-13: *The Message to the Church* *39*
Revelation 3:14-22: *The Church at Laodicea* *40*
    Revelation 3:14: *The Description of Christ* *40*
    Revelation 3:14-18: *The Message to the Messenger* *40*
    Revelation 3:19-22: *The Message to the Church* *41*

REVELATION 4:1-11: *BEHOLD, A THRONE* **43**

Revelation 4:1-3: *Presentation of The Throne* *43*
Revelation 4:4-11: *Proximity of the Throne* *44*

REVELATION 5:1-14: *WORTHY IS THE LAMB* **47**

Revelation 5:1: *The Book in God's Hand* **47**
Revelation 5:2-4: *The Need for One Worthy* *48*
Revelation 5:5-6: *The Lamb Standing* *49*
    Revelation 5:7-14: *The Lamb in Possession of the Book* *51*

THE SEVEN SEALS: *AN OVERVIEW* 53

Comparison of The Seals with Matthew 24 53
The Length and Timing of the Tribulation 54
Revelation 6:1-10: *The First Four Seals: The Four Horses of the Apocalypse* 55
Revelation 6:1-2: *The First Seal: The White Horse* 55
Revelation 6:3-4: *The second Seal: The Fiery Red Horse* 55
Revelation 6:5-6: *The Third Seal: The Black Horse* 56
Revelation 6:7-8: *The Fourth Seal: The Pale Horse* 56
Revelation 6:9-11: *The Fifth Seal* 57
Revelation 6:12-17: *The Sixth Seal* 58
Revelation 6:12-15: *The Physical Nature of the Sixth Seal* 59
Revelation 6:16-17: *The Knowledge of the Men of Earth* 59
Revelation 7:1-8: *The Sealing of the 144,000* 60
Revelation 7:9-17: *The Innumerable Multitude* 61
Revelation 7:9-12: *The Scene in Heaven* 61
Revelation 7:13: *The Important Question from the Elder* 62
Revelation 7:14: *The Answer from the Elder* 63
Revelation 7:15-17: *The Activity of The Multitude* 63
Revelation 8:1-5: *The Seventh Seal* 64
Revelation 8:1-5: *The Introduction* 64

REVELATION 8:6-9:21: *THE SEVEN TRUMPETS* 67

Revelation 8:7: *The First Trumpet* 67
Revelation 8:8-9: *The Second Trumpet* 69
Revelation 8:10-11: *The Third Trumpet* 69
Revelation 8:12-13: *The Fourth Trumpet* 70
Revelation 8:13: *The Triple Woe* 70
Revelation 9:1-12: *The Fifth Trumpet* 70
Revelation 9:13-21: *The Sixth Trumpet* 73

REVELATION 10:1-11:19: *A PARENTHETICAL STATEMENT* 75

Revelation 10:1-11: *A Strong Messenger With a Message* 75

Revelation 10:1-2: *The Mighty Angel* 75
Revelation 10:3-7: *The Mighty Message* 76
Revelation 10:8-11: *The Sweet and Sour Book* 78

Revelation 11:1-13: *The Two Witnesses* 79
Revelation 11:1-2: *The Times of the Gentiles* 79
Revelation 11:3-12: *The Two Witnesses* 80
Revelation 11:13-14: *The Completion of the Second Woe* 82

Revelation 11:15-19: *The Seventh Trumpet* 83
Revelation 11:15-17: *The Forecast of Reign* 83
Revelation 11:18-19: *The Response on Earth and Heaven* 85

REVELATION 12-15: *BEHIND THE SCENES* 89

Revelation 12:1-17: *The Sign and the War in Heaven* 90
Revelation 12:1-2: *The Woman* 90
Revelation 12:3-4: *Satan* 91
Revelation 12:5: *The Child* 92
Revelation 12:6: *The Woman, Revisited* 92
Revelation 12:7-9: *The War in Heaven* 93
Revelation 12:10-12a: *The Good Results of the War* 94
Revelation 12:12b-16: *The Bad Results of the War* 96
Revelation 12:17: *The Rest of the Jewish Nation* 98

Revelation 13:1-2: *The Beast out of the Sea* 98

Revelation 13:3: *The Wounded Head* 100
Revelation 13:4: *Future Worship* 101
Revelation 13:5-10: *The Blasphemous Reign* 101
Revelation 13:11: *The Second Beast* 104

Revelation 13:12-18: *The Work of the Second Beast* 105
Revelation 13:18: *The Mark of the Beast* 107

Revelation 14:1-20: *Looking Ahead* 107
Revelation 14:1-5: *The 144,000 in the Kingdom* 107
Revelation 14:6-7: *The Proclamation of the Everlasting Gospel* 110
Revelation 14:8: *The Proclamation of the Fall of Babylon* 111
Revelation 14:9-11: *The Proclamation of the Doom of the Followers of Antichrist* 111
Revelation 14:12-13: *The Patience of the Saints* 111
Revelation 14:14: *The Victorious Son of Man* 111

Revelation 14:15-16: *The Harvest of the Earth* 112
Revelation 14:17-20: *The Vine into the Winepress of Wrath* 113
Revelation 15:1-4: *The Great and Marvelous Sign* 113
Revelation 15:5-8: *The Seven Angels Introduced* 116

REVELATION 16:1-21: *THE SEVEN VIALS* 117

Revelation 16:1-11: *The First Five Vials* 117
Revelation 16:12-16: *The Sixth Vial* 118
Revelation 16:17-21: *The Seventh Vial* 120

REVELATION 17-18: *FUTURE BABYLON DESTROYED* 123

Revelation 17:1-2: *Invitation to View the Judgment* 123
Revelation 17:3-6: *The Woman* 124
Revelation 17:7-8: *The Angelic Explanation* 126
Revelation 17: 9-15: *A Further Explanation* 127
Revelation 17:16-18: *A final Explanation* 130
Revelation 18:1-3: *The Illuminating Angel* 131
Revelation 18:4-7: *Instructions for the Jews* 131
Revelation 18:8-19: *The Mourning of the Masses* 132
Revelation 18:20-24: *Heaven Rejoices* 134

REVELATION 19-20: *THE KING AND HIS KINGDOM* 135

Revelation 19:1-5: *Heaven Rejoices* 135
Revelation 19:6-10: *The Lamb, His Bride, and the Marriage Feast* 136
Revelation 19:11-16: *The Second Coming Seen* 139
Revelation 19:17-19: *The Battle of Armageddon* 142
Revelation 19:20-21: *The Outcome of the Battle* 142
Revelation 20:1-3: *The Binding of Satan* 143
Revelation 20:4-6: *The First Resurrection* 145

Revelation 20:7-10: *The Satanic Revolt* *146*
Revelation 20:11-15: *The Great White Throne Judgment* *148*

REVELATION 21-22: *THE NEW HEAVEN AND NEW EARTH* **151**
Revelation 21:1-5: *The New Revealed* *151*
Revelation 21:6-8: *A Word to the Wise Living in Tribulation* *152*
Revelation 21:9-27: *New Jerusalem Described* *153*
Revelation 22:1-6: *The Things Which Shall Quickly Come to Pass* *155*
Revelation 22:7-13: *The Coming Reward* *156*
Revelation 22:14-19: *Final Instructions* *157*
Revelation 22:20-21: *The Amen!* *158*

A NEW LOOK AT THE SEVEN CHURCHES OF REVELATION **159**
Revelation 1:1: *What the Book of Revelation is About* *159*
Revelation 1:10: *Where John is When he Writes* *160*
Is Revelation 1:19 an Outline of the Book? *161*
What Happens When You Apply Revelation 2-3 Today? *162*
    A Few Problematic Passages 162

PREFACE

The outlines of the book of Revelation in the following pages were originally given to students of the Randy White Ministries Online Bible Study which is presented each Thursday night to students from around the world. The outlines are a result of a diligent desire to study and present the Word of God in a verse-by-verse fashion. It is the author's prayer that these outlines can be used by pastors, Sunday School teachers, missionaries, and anyone who is wanting to understand the revelation contained in the Book of Revelation.

The notes are not exhaustive but should give the student a good concept of the "big picture" of the book as well as an understanding of specific issues. The interpretations are my own conclusions, and every student of the Word should question the assumptions to make sure that my conclusions are accurate and based on the Word from which they were derived. The only true source of authority comes from the text of the Scripture itself.

My perspective throughout the study is that of a classic dispensationalist, thus I believe in a pre-tribulational rapture of the church, which precedes the events of the book of Revelation.

Throughout the outline, I have attempted to consistently place in bold print the words that came from the King James Version of the Scripture.

It is my prayer that these outlines encourage you to the deeper study of the Word. Video of the original teaching of each session is available online at www.YouTube.com/randywhite, and is entitled the "Behold" series.

You are invited to join us on our online journey of Bible study each Thursday at 7:00 PM Mountain Time. For more information visit www.RandyWhiteMinistries.org.

Looking forward to His return!

Dr. Randy White

Taos, NM

INTRODUCTION OF THE REVELATION

Revelation 1:1-3: *The Prologue*

Revelation 1:1a: *The Content of the Revelation*

- The revelation (Apocalypse) is a **Revelation of Jesus Christ**, not a revelation of events yet to come.
  - Note the other uses of the word in relation to Jesus Christ to see that apocalypse is always a revealing of Jesus.
  - The revelation of Jesus Christ is a gift to Christ given by God in exchange for His propitiatory work on the cross. See Psalm 2:8 and Philippians 2:9.
- It is a mistake to view the book as a revelation *by* Jesus and not *of* Jesus (as seen in several poor translations).
- The Greek word *deí* is best translated "behoove," as only Young's literal does. In this light, the following, "soon take place" is not problematic.
- The Greek word *taxos* is the basis of the English "*tachometer*," which measures the speed of revolutions. The emphasis could be the speed at which the Revelation will unfold rather than the time-frame in which it will arrive.

Revelation 1:1b-2: *The Source of the Revelation*

- The Revelation is *of* Jesus and *communicated* by an Angel to John.
  - The word "communicated" is literally, **signified**.
    - The Angel did not communicate the revelation just in words, but in visions, so this word is precise.
  - Our English word *semantic* comes from this Greek root, *sema*.
    - Semantics is the study of the *meaning* of words.
    - Note that verse 2 speaks of what John **saw**.
- **His angel** - This is the angel assigned to Jesus Christ.
  - Seen also in Revelation 22:6 and 16.
  - Possibly the same angel who gives the trumpet call at the rapture
- The angel delivered the message through John.
  - **His servant John** - This clarifies which John it is; does any other John than the apostle and author of the Gospel of John fit this description?
  - In Greek, verse 2 speaks of "the logos of God," which is exactly what John wrote in the Gospel. See also 1 John 1:1-4.

Revelation 1:3: *The Blessing of the Revelation*

- There is a threefold requirement: read, hear, and heed. In Revelation 22:7, 10, and 18 the emphasis is on "heed."
- The requirement was toward **the things which are written**.
  - In verse 1 the vision was **signified**.
  - In verse 2 John testified all he **saw**.
  - But it is the written *words*, not the *sight* that we read, hear, and heed.

- Beware of interpretations of the book that abuse the plain meaning of words.

▸ **The time is at hand**

- He did not say the *chronos* is near, but the *kairos*.
  - Chronologically, the time was far.
  - In Acts 1:7, we are told that we are not to know either the *chronos* or the *kairos*.
- This statement, as well as **shortly** in verse 1 most certainly speaks of the *certainty* and *imminence* of the Lord's return.
  - Such imminence demands a pre-tribulation rapture because the events which will unfold in the Revelation give a clear chronology.

Revelation 1:4-7: *The Greeting*

Revelation 1:4: *The Penman and the Recipients*

▸ **To the seven churches –**

- **Seven** is the number of spiritual perfection or completion.
- It can be seen as 4 + 3 (creation plus spirit), 5+2 (grace plus witness), 6+1 (man plus God)

Revelation 1:4b-5a: *The Author*

▸ The Father: That is, from Yahweh, the I AM.

▸ **The seven Spirits**: A difficult phrase, but undoubtedly a reference to the Holy Spirit. Perhaps Zechariah 4:2-6 is in view.

▸ The Son: Jesus Christ, (who is being revealed) is described by 4 words:

- **Faithful**
- **Witness** (or possibly, "**faithful witness**")
- **First begotten of the dead**
- **Prince of the kings of the earth** (a role which He does not fully express in our age, but will - Revelation 17:14).

Revelation 1:5b-7: *The Doxology*

▶ The Blood of Jesus – **in his own blood**

- Note a textual variant. **Washed** is in the *Textus Receptus*, and is the preferred reading.
- While we are *released* from our sins, it is the blood that *washes* us. See 1 John 1:7
- See Hebrews 9:22. Much of Christianity has a bloodless message of salvation. Love, commitment, prayer, obedience, etc. do not save us. His blood alone can cleanse us.

▶ **Kings and priests**

- *Textus Receptus* is **kings** rather than "kingdom" (also in Rev. 5:10).
  - The dominion role of man will be ultimately restored in and through Christ.
  - The present tense speaks of our spiritual reality, but the physical reality is not delivered. Note that Revelation 5:10 is in the present but is clearly talking about people in the future.
  - The textual variant is important because we *are* **kings** but *we are not* a Kingdom. The Kingdom is yet future.

▶ Verse 7 is about the Second Coming (the apocalypse) not the rapture.

Revelation 1:8 : *The Declaration of God the Father*

- ▸ The Textus Receptus (KJV) adds **the beginning and the end**. Specifically, the *arche* and the *telos*, the *origin* and the *completion*.

- ▸ The Critical text adds the word "God." However, in light of the usage of the same phrase in Revelation 11:17, this can only be God the Father. The Alpha and Omega as the Father aligns with Revelation 21:6, and in Revelation 22:13 is used of Jesus.

Revelation 1:9-11: *The Context and the Instruction*

Revelation 1:9: *From Whom, Where, and Why*

- ▸ John is the **brother** and **companion**
  - In **tribulation,** but not "The Tribulation"
    - ○ Even in a preterist view, it hasn't yet begun.
    - ○ The phrase "*τη θλιψει*" *(thilipsis)* is used 7 times in the New Testament, and never means anything other than «tribulations or afflictions.»
    - ○ An interpretation that viewed this as "The Tribulation" would be incompatible with the words of Paul in 1 Thessalonians 1:10, and other passages.
  - **In the Kingdom,** but not physically in the Kingdom.
    - ○ Because the Kingdom only comes after the tribulation, John cannot be saying that he is currently a partaker in the Kingdom (and if he is, who wants that kind of Kingdom?) Rather, he is a **brother and companion…in the kingdom.**
    - ○ John speaks in the same manner as Paul in 2 Timothy 2:12.

- In **patience,** but not his own
  - *Hupomoné* is associated with hope (1 Thess. 1:3) and refers to that quality of character which does not allow one to surrender to circumstances or succumb under trial. (Zodhiates, Spiros. *The complete word study dictionary: New Testament* 2000)
  - Note: This *hupomone* is not *our patience* but Christ's, and John says he is a **companion.** Note Hebrews 12:2 concerning the endurance of Christ.
  - The Textus Receptus (KJV) does not have the word "in," (as in NASB), and only the **patience** is "of" Jesus.
- John is imprisoned as a result of holding to the Word and his continued testimony. Compare with Revelation 6:9

Revelation 1:10a: *John, Taken Away and Hearing a Voice*

- **In the Spirit on the Lord's Day** - Does this mean that John was in a spiritual ecstatic experience on Sunday? Or that he was *spiritually* (not physically) taken to the Lord's Day?'
  - Should this be **in the Spirit** or simply, in spirit? Compare to Matthew 22:43 and John 1:24 for a rendering of the phrase that simply implies "non-physical."
    - Note that there is no definite article (which is often implied in Greek, so may or may not be inserted into the English translation).
    - Either interpretation is possible.
    - Note also that KJV is inconsistent when compared to Revelation 4:2, 17:3, and 21:10, which are the only other times the phrase is used in Revelation.

- The reader should always beware of capitalization for Deity in any English translation.
- Concerning **on the Lord's day**, most translators (and some translations) make the assumption that this is speaking of Sunday.
  - Using the principle of allowing Scripture to interpret itself, this is suspicious. There is no reference to Sunday as **the Lord's day**, but many references to *the day of the Lord*, which is that period of judgment at the end of days.
  - It is my belief that this verse tells us that John was spiritually (not physically) taken forward in time to the Day of the Lord, which is given by God to Jesus, and John is going to record what happens, in advance.

Revelation 1:10b-11: *The Instruction*

▶ **A great voice, as of a trumpet** - Because John comes to give this voice a new description, either

- Verse 8 is a preview of what was actually said later [this is the position of the KJV, judging from its red letter edition], or
- A new and different voice from verse 8, namely, the voice of Jesus is in verse 11 and the voice of the Father in verse 8.
- The slightly different rendering of **the beginning and ending** (v. 8) to **the first and last** (v. 11, KJV), along with the reference to **the Almighty** in verse 8, is an indication that this is the first-time John has heard the voice of Jesus, having previously heard the voice of the Father.
- Whichever interpretation one takes, this voice in verse 11 is clarified as that of the Son in verse 12 and following.

- **I am the Alpha and Omega the first and the last** - Due to a textual variant, it is essential to use the KJV or NKJV on verse 11.
  - Note that John was to **write in a book**.
  - It is this book that we study, and must limit our "hearing God's voice" to this book. Only John had the blessed privilege of hearing the voice of the Lord.

Revelation 1:12-16: *The Sight John Beheld*

The Fourfold Sight

- The seven lampstands (v. 12)
- The Savior (vv. 13-15)
- The seven stars (v. 16a)
- The sharp sword (v. 16b)
  - The two-edged sword is seen again in the letter to Pergamum as well as in Revelation 19:15, 21 (at the Second Coming).
  - This sword is stronger than the "sharp, two-edged sword" of the Bible, which is a *machairon* (from which we get *machette)*, a small, personal sword. This sword is a *romphia*, a large sword worn over the shoulder.
- Note: Seven is a number for *spiritual perfection* and is used over 50 times in the book of Revelation

>  **Note:**
> *Principles of Interpretation in Revelation*
>
> - The only sure interpretation is one given by the text itself, or in an exact use of the term in other Scriptures.
> - Meanings drawn from implication may or may not be true, and must be treated as conjecture.
> - If a meaning seems to be true but is not clearly defined, then ask:
>   - Is there a need to determine a meaning?
>   - Is the conjectured meaning true the first time the word or phrase appears in Scripture?
>   - Is the conjectured meaning ever contradicted in Scripture?

The Description of the Savior

▶ The Description:
- Like a son of man
- Clothed in a robe reaching to the feet
- Girded with a golden sash
- Head and hair **white like wool** / snow
- Eyes of a flaming fire
- Feet of burnished bronze
- Voice like **the sound of many waters**

- The meaning: not revealed. Likely simply a physical description of the Glorious Risen Savior. There is no need to read meaning into each element of the description.

Revelation 1:17-20: *The Comfort and Instruction to John*

Revelation 1:17: *Jesus as the First and the Last*

- Earlier the Father was the *arche* and *telos*, **the beginning and the end**.
- Now, Jesus is the *protos* and the *eschatos*, **the first and the last**.
- On both occasions, one is foundational to the other, the first being *spiritual* and the latter being *substantive*.
- Note the comparative use of these in the book:
  - *Arche* and *telos*:
    - Revelation 1:8 - of the Father
    - Revelation 22:13 - of the Father, together with the Son
  - *Protos* and *eschatos*:
    - Revelation 1:11 - of the Son
    - Revelation 1:17 - of the Son
    - Revelation 2:8 - of the Son
    - Revelation 22:13 - of the Son, together with the Father

Revelation 1:18: *Jesus as Ruler of Life*

- It appears that the keys given to Peter have now been returned to Jesus, if **the keys of hell and of death** are the same as the "keys to the Kingdom." In either case, neither Peter nor his successor has the keys to death and Hades today.

Revelation 1:19-20: *The Instruction to Write and a Mystery Revealed*

- A **mystery** in the Bible is that which was previously unknown but has now been revealed. It can only become known by revelation. After the revelation, there is no need for speculation of any kind.

REVELATION 2-3:
THE LETTERS TO THE SEVEN CHURCHES

Interpretations of the Seven Churches

The Historical Interpretation
- The seven churches were seven literal churches in John's Day.
- The messages to the seven churches are specific to the particular church, but dynamically applicable to all churches.

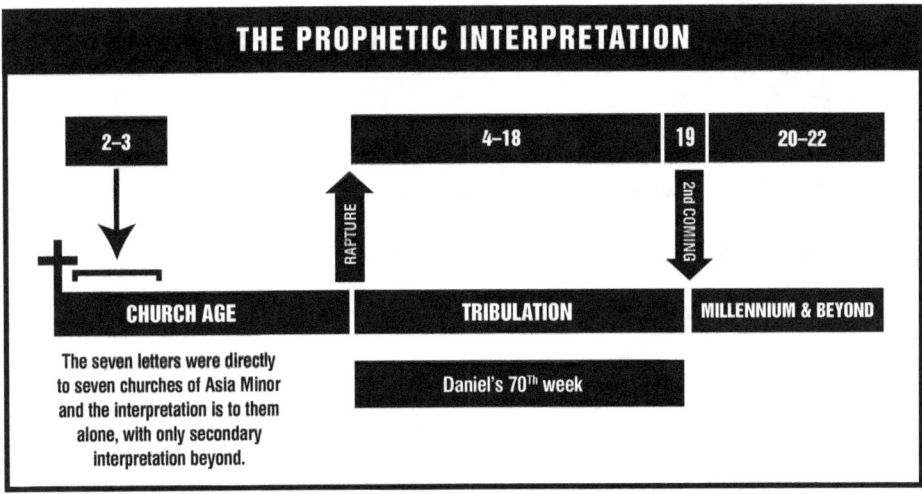

The Prophetic Interpretation

- The seven churches were seven literal churches in John's Day.

- The messages were specific to the particular church and dynamically applicable to all churches.

- The messages also have an implicit prophecy giving a testimony of the history of the church.

  - This is a dangerous method of interpretation, but not an unacceptable method.

    - Implicit prophecy is only seen perfectly in the "rear view mirror."

    - Psalm 22 is implicit prophecy

    - With Psalm 22, we have a Biblical key to interpretation (the fulfillment through the crucifixion of Christ). With Revelation 2-3, we do not have that Biblical key.

  - Any prophetic interpretation must be given for insight, not for doctrine.

- The typical prophetic interpretation:

  - Ephesus: *the apostolic church* | 33 AD to 100 AD
  - Smyrna: *the post-apostolic church* | 100-300
  - Pergamum: *the Constantinian church* | 300-600
  - Thyatira: *the Catholic church* | 600-1450
  - Sardis: *the reformation church* | 1450-1700
  - Philadelphia: *the missionary church* | 1700-1950
  - Laodicea: *the contemporary church* | 1950-present

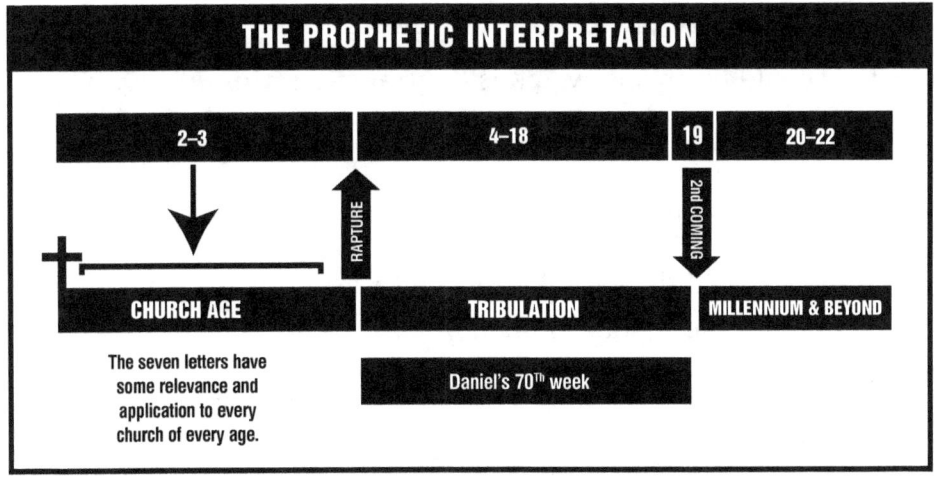

The Futurist Interpretation

▸ The seven churches were not necessarily churches in John's day.

▸ The messages should not be applied to a historic congregation nor to any church today (any more than the remainder of the book of Revelation).

▸ The churches are seven future Jewish assemblies, and the entire book is *futurist*.

▸ *Note: See Appendix 1 for "A New Look at the Seven Churches"*

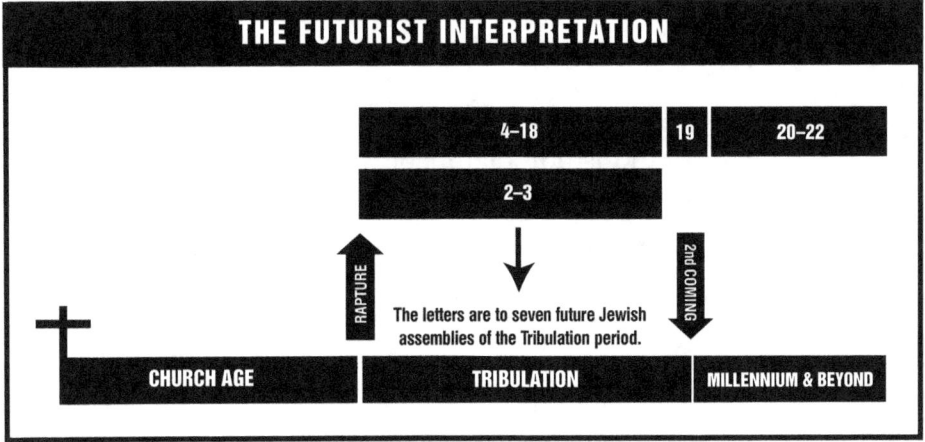

Who Are the "Angels" of the Churches?

- They could be angels, which is the **transliteration** of *angelos*
- They could be messengers, which is the **translation** of *angelos*
- The problem with the angelic view: (*Theodore Zahn*)
  - Why would the letter be written to a spiritual being and given through the agency of man?
  - Why would the angels receive rebuke and accusation of sinful conduct?

Revelation 2:1-7: *The Church at Ephesus*

Revelation 2:1: *The Description of Christ*

- The One who holds the seven stars in His right hand
  - If these messengers are interpreted as pastors, then they are held in His hand. However, this word for held is an almost violent word, used here more in the sense of being held accountable than held in protection.
- The one who walks among the seven golden lampstands
  - The seven golden lampstands are the churches (Rev. 1:20). Note that a lampstand is not a lamp, but that which holds the lamp (Matt. 4:15). When the church tries to BE the light, it fails. The church LIFTS UP the light. The light of the world is Jesus.

Revelation 2:2-6: *The Message to the Messenger*

- **I know…**
  - There are three Greek words for knowledge.
    - *Ginosko* - to know by experience
    - *Epistamai*: to know by proximity (see the use of both terms in 1 Cor. 13:12)
    - *Eido*: to know with the mind's eye, a mental perception.
  - Here, Christ knows in His mind, as in Matthew 6:8.
- Commendations:
  - Works, labour, and patience (v. 2, 3)
  - Intolerance of evil men (v. 2)
    - The Greek word for tolerate / bear is *bastazo* is the root of our English "basis." Literally, "you give no footing to evil men."
  - Testing of apostles
    - The apostolic test was to have received instruction directly from Jesus Christ, with no intermediary.
  - A hatred for the **deeds of the Nicolaitanes**
    - Literally, the "followers of Nicolas."
      - The name means "victory people," perhaps an indicator of their love for power, victory, and achievement.
- Condemnations
  - Having left the first love.
    - The first love of the Ephesian pastor had been left, and remedy was to remember **therefore from whence thou art fallen, and repent, and do the first works.**

- It seems that the first love was a work, not a Person. The pastor was reprimanded for losing a love for *something* not *someone*.
- Since the pastor was already commended for his works and labor (v. 2), this is some kind of deed that he *first* did, but no longer does.
- The most likely possibility (drawn from extra-Biblical sources) is the support for Jewish believers.

Revelation 2:7: *The Message to the Church*

▸ In each letter, a portion is given to the pastor, and a portion to the church.

▸ The reader can discern the difference by watching closely the use of 2nd person singular for the pastor and 2nd person plural or 3rd person singular for the church.

▸ The overcomer is the one with the ultimate victory, a play on words from the *Nicolaitans*. The true Victory People are described in 1 John 5:4-5.

▸ The overcomer will be granted to eat of the tree of life in the **paradise of God**. This phrase is used in two other places of Scripture, and refers to Heaven, prior to the establishment of the Kingdom. See Luke 23:43 and 2 Corinthians 12:4

Revelation 2:8-11: *The Church at Smyrna*

Revelation 2:8: *The Description of Christ*

▸ The word *smyrna* means *myrrh*. The same Greek word is used in Matthew 2:11, Mark 15:23, and John 19:39.

- Christ is presented as **the first and the last**
  - *Protos* and *eschatos*
  - This is a phrase used of God the Son. See note on Revelation 1:17.
- Christ is the one who "became dead" (literal translation) and lived.
  - John 10:18 sheds light on the middle voice of the word.
  - Middle voice is something done to oneself, translated in the active, not passive.

Revelation 2:9-11: *The Message to the Messenger*
- I know…
  - **Works, and tribulation, and poverty** (v. 9)
    - Note: Works is not included in modern translations
    - Tribulation and poverty are both strong selections of words
      - Not afflictions but tribulations
      - Not going without but being a beggar
  - **The blasphemy of them which say they are Jews, and are not**
    - The blasphemy itself: they claim to be Jews
      - The truth: they are not Jews at all
      - Biblically, to be Jewish, one must be a descendent of Jacob
    - This Scripture is notoriously interpreted *theologically* rather than *grammatically*.
      - Furthermore, the theology is wrong! It is the theology of *suppressionism* (replacement theology).
      - Consistency demands that Revelation 2:2 be

interpreted the same ways as Revelation 2:9, yet very few commentators are consistent.

- The commendation:
  - Do not fear the things which you will suffer (v. 10)
  - Be faithful unto death, and receive a crown of life (v. 11)

Revelation 2:10-11: *The Message to the Church*

- The devil will cast some of you into prison (v. 10)
  - You will be tried
  - You will have tribulation for 10 days.
    - While we a prone to take this figuratively, there is no place in the book of Revelation where a time period is given in figurative manner.
    - Caution: many commentators, looking for a historical reference, have allegorized these 10 days, making up every type of application. It is best to take this as either a reference to a future event or an unknown even in the past.
- The overcomer will not be hurt by the second death.
  - The first death may overtake the overcomer, but the second death will have no power.

Revelation 2:12-17: *The Church at Pergamos*

Revelation 2:12: *The Description of Christ*

- Pergamum = *per* (through) *gamos* (marriage)

- Christ presents Himself as Warrior, with the sharp, two-edged sword used in battle (Rev. 19:15)

Revelation 2:13-16: *The Message to the Messenger*

- **Where thou dwellest, even where Satan's seat is** (v. 13) This is simple acknowledgment, subtle commendation, or strong condemnation.
- The fact that the Pastor works and dwells (KJV only) where Satan's throne is likely seen as an acknowledgment of the difficult circumstances of Pergamos.
- We do not have definitive interpretation for the identity of **Satan's seat,** but it is certainly not literal. It could be a future reference to an as-yet-unfulfilled prophecy of a ruling center for the Antichrist.
- The Pastor is clearly commended because **thou holdest fast my name** (v. 13). This is the same word for hold used in verse 1, it is the strongest word for hold available. This Pastor is commended for his grip on the name of Jesus.
- Even in the days of the Martyrdom of Antipas, the pastor did not let go of the name of Jesus.
  - Nothing further is known of Antipas beyond the information given here. Tradition says that he was burned alive under the reign of Domitian.
  - The words of praise for Antipas are beyond compare - note Revelation 1:5.
- There was a clear condemnation also: he allowed false teaching to remain in the church.
  - In English, it is hard to tell if the condemnation of verse 14 is against people who do three things or if it is all connected. In

Greek, it is a single unit, Balaam having taught Balak to entice Israel to eat things sacrificed to idols and to commit immorality. See Numbers 25:2 and 31:16.

- Unlike the Ephesian pastor, the Pergamum pastor allowed the teaching of the Nicolaitans.

Revelation 2:17: *The Message to the Church*

- **Hidden manna**: Possibly a reference to the manna of the Ark of the Covenant, hidden since the days of the Babylonian captivity.

- **A white stone**: Interpretations of this white stone are so numerous as to make this beyond interpretation, other than to know that it appears to be a blessing. Since Scripture does not define it, and since there is no clear extra-Biblical definition, it is best left without interpretation.

- **A new name**: There is a mystery yet to be revealed in the new name. See Revelation 19:12.

Revelation 2:18-29: *The Church at Thyatira*

Revelation 2:18: *The Description of Christ*

- This is the only description in which the phrase **"Son of God"** is used.

- Since the phrase about the eyes and feet are also used in Revelation 1:13-16, the **"Son of God"** usage here removes any doubt that chapter 1 is about Jesus Christ.

Revelation 2:19-23a: *The Message to the Messenger*

- **I know…**
  - Your works (practical works – *erga*)
  - Your love (*agape*)
  - Your service (*diakanon*)
  - Your faith (*pistis*)
  - Your endurance (*hupomeno*)
- **The commendation:**
  - Your last works are more than your first works
- **The condemnation: They put up with Jezebel**
  - Toleration is not always commendable. The word "tolerate" (NASB) / **sufferest** (KJV) is often translated "forgive."
  - Jezebel is either a real name or a pseudonym, but the reality of the person should not be questioned.
  - As in Revelation 2:2 and 2:9, there is a verbal claim that has no physical justification.
  - The condemnation concerning Jezebel
    - The pastor forgives her teaching
    - The pastor forgives her misleading Christ's slaves to commit fornication
    - The pastor forgives her misleading Christ's slaves to eat things sacrificed to idols (1 Cor. 10:28)
  - Direct words about the woman and her disciples:
    - Jesus gave her time to repent, but she did not.
      - Textual variant. Critical text adds, "she does not want

to repent" rather than **she repented not.**

- ○ Jesus will **cast her into a bed**
  - ◆ NASB adds, "*of sickness*"
  - ◆ Nothing inherent in the word requires sickness. It could be that Christ gives her up to immorality.
- ○ It is possible that Christ casts **her…and them who commit adultery with her** into a bed, which then is cast into great tribulation
- ○ She has had time, and her followers still have time: **except they repent of their deeds.**

Revelation 2:23b-29: *The Message to the Church*

▶ The repayment according to deeds (v. 23) is in the plural, and is a message to the church.

▶ The message of putting up with Jezebel was given solely to the pastor. To the church He says, **"I will put upon you none other burden"** (KJV).

▶ The church's further instruction:

- Hold fast to what you have, overcome, and keep Christ's deeds

▶ The promise to the church:

- Authority and rule over the nations
- The *Morning Star* (doubtless a reference to the appearance of Christ) (Rev. 22:16)

Revelation 3:1-6: *The Church at Sardis*

Revelation 3:1: *The Description of Christ*
- The one who has the Seven Spirits of God and the seven stars, which are the pastors.

Revelation 3:1-4: *The Message to the Messenger*
- I Know…
  - **Thy works**
  - The reputation of life
  - The deadness of the pastor (no doubt of his spiritual vitality)
- The Commendation:
  - Verse 4 - This pastor does not really get a commendation. The closest it comes is that there are a few within the church who still remain faithful.
  - Note that the faithfulness of a member is not dependent upon the spiritual life of the pastor.
- The Condemnation:
  - **Be watchful**, or WAKE UP!
  - Your works are not complete, yet you are letting them die
  - If the pastor does not remember and repent, the Lord will come upon him suddenly, as a thief, and the pastor will not be ready. Compare 1 Thessalonians 5:1-4

Revelation 3:5-6: *The Message to the Church*
- The overcomer will be dressed in white, priestly robes.

- ▸ The overcomer's name is safely in the book of life.
- ▸ Jesus will confess the name of the overcomer before the Father and His angels.

Revelation 3:7-13: *The Church at Philadelphia*

Revelation 3:7: *The Description of Christ*

- ▸ Unlike the other churches, this description is entirely new, not found in chapter 1.
- ▸ The person of Christ: Holy and true
- ▸ The possession of Christ: the key of David (compare Is. 22:20-25)

Revelation 3:8-11: *The Message to the Messenger*

- ▸ The message to this pastor does not fit the pattern used in other churches (I know/ commendation / condemnation).
- ▸ Because Christ knows the works of this pastor:
  - Behold: an open door (v. 8)
    - The open door is not defined in the passage, and any definition is speculation, though the door is almost certainly not literal.
    - The door has been set before them because:
      - The pastor has a little power (presumably spiritual power, but not defined)
      - With this power, the pastor kept God's Word
      - With this power, keeping God's Word, the pastor did not deny Christ's name

- Behold: a synagogue of Satan (v. 9)
  - This synagogue is **of Satan** and made of those who declare themselves to be Jews even though they are not Jews; they are liars.
  - These liars will be forced to:
    - Come and worship in the sight of the pastor
    - Recognize the love of Christ for this pastor
- Behold: I am coming quickly (v. 10-11)
  - Verse 11 is the result of verse 10 (rather than verse 10 being the cause of verse 9).
  - The coming appearance (v. 11)
    - **I come quickly** (emphasis added; an adverb)
    - Hold fast: there is a chance of losing the *crown* (not the salvation)
  - The pastor's action: Keeping the word of Christ's endurance
  - The result: Being kept from the hour of testing that will come.
    - This testing will come upon the whole earth
    - This time is to test **them that dwell upon the earth (v.10)**
      - ✓ This phrase is only used of the time of Tribulation
      - ✓ See Revelation 6:10; 8:13; 11:10; 13:8, 14; 17:8

Revelation 3:12-13: *The Message to the Church*

▶ To the overcomer, Christ will:
  - Make him a pillar in the Temple, where he will dwell forever

- Write upon him
  - The name of God
  - The name of the New Jerusalem (the Bride of Christ)
  - The new name of Christ
▸ The one with ears, should hear!

Revelation 3:14-22: *The Church at Laodicea*

Revelation 3:14: *The Description of Christ*

▸ **The Amen**: A Hebrew word meaning *established and verified*.

▸ The Witness who is faithful and true

▸ The Beginning of the creation of God

- This is not in the sense of the "first thing of God's creation," but the "source" of the creation of God.

Revelation 3:14-18: *The Message to the Messenger*

▸ I Know…

- **Thy works**
- *That you are neither cold nor hot* (I would rather you be one or the other)
  - No morality is assigned to cold or hot, but this passage is clearly speaking figuratively of lack of conviction.

▸ The Commendation:

- None given

- The Condemnation:
  - **I will going to spue thee out of my mouth** – verse 16
  - The counsel:
    - Buy gold, to be rich
    - Buy white clothes, to be covered
    - Anoint your eyes, to see

Revelation 3:19-22: *The Message to the Church*

- I rebuke and discipline those I love, therefore be zealous and repent.
- I stand at the door and knock: I will come in if the door is opened.
- The overcomer will sit with me in my throne

REVELATION 4:1-11:
BEHOLD, A THRONE

Revelation 4:1-3: *Presentation of The Throne*

▶ Verse 1
- These **things** were indicated in Revelation 1:19. Since the entirety of the revelation is in "the day of the Lord," these **things** are both future and take place sometime after the seven churches are established.
- The door was already opened when John looked.
- If this is the voice of Revelation 1:10, then this quote should be in red letters.

▶ Verse 2
- **In the spirit** - The Greek has no definite article. The capitalization of "Spirit" (NASB) is questionable.
- "a throne was standing" (NASB) - KJV is more accurate with "**was set**." The word is the same word used for burial (and the English word *cemetery* comes from this Greek word, *keimai*). This is a verb, indicating that something had been set for the occasion.
- **One sat on the throne** - The "one" is not in the Greek but is almost required for English.

- The picture is of a throne being carried in, with one sitting on the throne, and John watching the action.
- God on His throne is a picture of judgment. Compare Psalm 11:4-7 to this chapter.

▶ Verse 3

- Jasper – a translucent stone (such as a diamond)
- Sardis – a red stone (such as a ruby)
- Rainbow – The Greek word is *iris*, from which we get the name for the colored circle around the pupil of the eye, as well as for "iridescent" and "iridium." This rainbow is also seen in Ezekiel 1:28.

Revelation 4:4-11: *Proximity of the Throne*

▶ Verse 4

- Twenty-four elders – Angelic or human?
  - Aspects in favor of the elders being human:
    - The twelve apostles will sit upon thrones in the earthly Kingdom (Mt. 19:28)
    - There will be "saints who judge the world" who sit on thrones (Dan. 7:22, 1 Cor. 6:2, Rev. 20:4)
  - Aspects in favor of the elders being angelic:
    - It appears that these 24 Elders will worship God the Father **for ever and ever**, making it impossible for them to leave the throne room of Heaven for the throne room of earth.

- They present the prayers of God's people to the Father (Rev. 5:8), which seems to be an angelic role in Revelation 8:3.
- They speak to John, something only done by angelic beings in Revelation (Rev. 5:5)
- They appear to be counted with the angelic beings (Rev. 5:11)
- They distinguish themselves from the bond-servants of God (Rev. 11:18)
  - 1 Chronicles 28:11-14 suggests that the 24 courses of the Priesthood were set up after this pattern.
- Verse 5
  - These are not "menorahs" but the lamp, which sits atop the menorah (Ex. 25:37).
  - In Zechariah 4:10 and Revelation 5:6 the lamps, which are the Spirits, are also **the eyes of the Lord.**
- Verse 6
  - Comparing with Ezekiel 1:5-14 and Ezekiel 10:20, these are Cherubim (also seen in Genesis 3:24. These living creatures are held distinct from angels) (Rev. 5:11)
- Verse 7
  - KJV translates *zoan* as **beast**, NASB as "creature." These are clearly indescribable.
  - Since they are *cherubim*, a word that is always untranslated, it would not be out of question to simply call these *zoan*.
- Verse 10

- The Greek *proskuneo* is literally, "toward a dog," giving reference to the manner in which a dog would, with loyalty, kiss his master's feet.
- The throne room in heaven is one of worship, even in the face of the coming judgment.

REVELATION 5:1-14:
WORTHY IS THE LAMB

Revelation 5:1: *The Book in God's Hand*

- ▸ The book is in the **right hand** - From *dexios* from which we get *dexterity* and *ambidextrous* (*ambi=both, dextrous=right hands*).

- ▸ **Him that sat on the throne** - This is a reference to the Father (Rev. 1:4). It is Biblically incorrect to refer to Christ "on His throne." Anytime we read of One of the Trinity on the throne it is either God the Father or a future event of God the Son. For examples of Christ and His throne see the following:
  - Where He is now--Hebrews 8:1, 12:2
  - Where He will be in the future-- Matthew 19:28, 25:31; Luke 1:32; Revelation 3:21

- ▸ **A book** - The Greek word *biblion* is often translated "book," but is more accurately a *volume*, the word not designating form at all. Therefore, this was likely a *scroll* that contained a *biblion* of information.
  - In the Septuagint, *biblion* is used in Isaiah 34:4, but clearly a *scroll* is in view.

- What is this book?
  - Isaiah 34:16 speaks of **the book of the LORD** and the assurance that what is written in it will happen, and the context is the judgment of the nations at the end of days.
  - Ezekiel saw a similar book in Ezekiel 2:9-10, written on both sides and **written therein lamentations, and mourning, and woe.**
  - This is the intensified version of the word *sealed*, literally, *ultimately sealed*.
- The non-intensified form is found in Revelation 7 (the sealing of the 144,000) and Revelation 20 (the 1,000 year sealing of Satan).
- This is the only time this form of the word is used in the New Testament.
- Combine with this the seven-count of seals and the picture is given that there is no hope of opening this book without Divine intervention.

Revelation 5:2-4: *The Need for One Worthy*

▶ A *strong* angel - This angel is not necessarily "stronger," but is **strong**.

- The word can be physical strength (Lk. 11:22), logical or rhetorical strength (2 Cor. 10:10), or positional strength (Rev. 18:10).
- An angel of strength is seen in Revelation 10:1 and 18:21.
- Psalm 103:20 speaks of the strength of angels in a general manner.

- Perhaps this angel's strength is noted because of the announcement he is about to give.
- "Break its seals" (NASB) is a poor translation. KJV is correct with **loose**.
- Verse 3 is, in a sense, a summary of the plot of the Old Testament, as the people of God were looking for the One who was worthy.
- Verse 4 - Just as "all creation groans under the curse," John was groaning and weeping because the only hope for rightful ownership restored seems to be gone.

Revelation 5:5-6: *The Lamb Standing*

- **The Lion** – verse 5
  - The "**Lion**" overcame *in order to* open the book and **loose the seven seals** (*loose* is omitted from the Critical Text).
  - We should not forget that the purpose of the resurrection is not just the "here and now" nor is it just about that which is "spiritual." Rather, the resurrection must be fundamentally understood to be *for the purpose* **of** opening this scroll and breaking its seals.
  - Today, the Lamb awaits the day of opening, which is "the day of the Lord" (or, "**the Lord's day**," in Rev. 1:10).
- **A Lamb** – verse 6
  - Where is the Lamb?
    - NASB uses "between," rather than the accurate **in the midst of**.
    - Since NASB uses *between* they have had to make the four living creatures a parenthetical statement.

- Rather, the language suggests the Lamb standing in the midst of three things: the creatures, the throne, and the elders.
- Since chapter 4 presents the throne surrounded by the creatures, which are surrounded by the elders, the word *between* or *in the middle of* is physically impossible. However, the Greek *mesos* is simply "amongst" or "in the midst," and does not imply *middle* or *between*.

- Why is the Lamb *standing*?
  - The fact that the Lamb (clearly the Lord Jesus Christ) is standing is significant.
  - We have seen Him always *sitting* at the right hand of the Father, except on one occasion, Acts 7:55-56. In that passage, Stephen asked, in effect, for the Lord to "be seated" and "stand not this sin against them," (literal rendering of Acts 7:60).
  - In the book of Hebrews, Jesus finished His work and "sat down."
  - In the Psalms, when a time of judgment is coming, the Lord would "rise up" (Ps. 7:6, 9:19, etc.).

- The Lamb's description –
  - Not standing "as if slain" (NASB) but "as slain." The Lamb is "standing slain," and about to reap the rewards for His obedience unto death.
  - Horns are a symbol of governmental power (Dan. 8:19-22).
  - Eyes are a symbol of knowledge.
    - In Zechariah 3:9, the eyes are set upon **one Stone** (the Cornerstone).

- In Zechariah 4:10, the seven eyes **shall rejoice, and shall see the plummet** (of judgment).
  - The eyes are the seven Spirits of God, which have been sent into all the earth. There are three possible interpretations:
    - This is the Holy Spirit, and the *seven* is purely symbolic.
    - There are literally seven *spirits*, but they are not the Holy Spirit, who is one Person.
      - ✓ The interpretive rule used in Matthew 12:45 needs to be used here as well (interpret both literally or both symbolically).
      - ✓ If a fallen angel can be called a *pneumata* why can't an unfallen angel be called the same?
    - This is a reference to Isaiah the seven-fold spirit of Isaiah 11:2.

Revelation 5:7-14: *The Lamb in Possession of the Book*

▶ When the Lamb takes the book, all creation will rejoice!

▶ The **New Song** (vv. 9-10)

- The question of a pronoun
  - "**They**" is most likely "the saints," the ones who are "purchased," etc. This is not the song of the creatures and elders, but of the saints.
  - The KJV / Textus Receptus uses the personal pronoun "**us**" in verses 9-10, while the Critical Text uses "them" (implied in v. 9 and explicit in v. 10). If it is the saints singing, then "**us**" makes perfect sense. When assuming the Creatures/Elders are singing, "them" is a necessity, since the creatures cannot be redeemed.

- The song itself:
  - Verse 9 speaks of one aspect of the rejoicing of the creatures: the *worth* of the Lamb based on His shed blood. Verse 12 speaks of the second necessary aspect, the *power* of the Lamb to take possession of His people / inheritance.
  - The Lamb has "**redeemed** [the saints] **to God**," "**out of**" (*ek*) every tribe, etc.
    - This is likely the song of the Jewish saints (pre-AD 70 Jewish believers), they were redeemed **out of** the various nations of the earth, where they had been scattered.
    - These saints have now been dead, mostly by martyrdom, for almost 2,000 years, and their prayers (of that day) are still being held before the Father.
  - Verse 10 - The KJV is correct in **Kings** not *Kingdom* (see notes on Rev. 1:6).
- All Creation sings (vv. 11-14)
  - Verse 13, "**every creature…**" is not a problem for us because we are reminded that John is seeing that which is exclusively in the future, when "**every knee should bow…and that every tongue should confess that Jesus Christ is Lord**" (Phil. 2:10-11).

THE SEVEN SEALS: *AN OVERVIEW*

Comparison of The Seals with Matthew 24

- First seal (vv. 1-2), Matthew 24:4-5
- Second, third, and fourth seals (vv. 3-8), Matthew 24:6-7
- Fifth seal (vv. 9-11), Matthew 24:8-28
- Sixth seal (vv. 12-17), Matthew 24:29-30
- Sealing of the 144,000 (Rev. 7:1-8), Matthew 24:31

COMPARISON OF THE SEALS WITH MATTHEW 24

MATTHEW 24	SEALS OF REVELATION
Matthew 24:4–5	First seal (Rev. 6:1–2)
Matthew 24:6–7	Second, third and fourth seals (Rev. 6:3–8)
Matthew 24:8–28	Fifth seal (Rev. 6:9–11)
Matthew 24:29–30 (Also Joel 2:28,31)	Sixth seal (Rev. 6:12–17)
Matthew 24:31-51	Sealing of the 144,000 (Rev. 7:1 – 19:21)

70th Week of Daniel

The Length and Timing of the Tribulation

- Without doubt, the length of the "Day of Jacob's Trouble" is seven years.

  - Revelation 13:5 – the Antichrist has a discernable portion of his reign of 42 months. Prior to this time, he is at work but his work may be indiscernible with any "beyond shadow of a doubt" proof.

  - Numerous Biblical indicators break these 42 months into two halves of 1,260 days.

- Almost without exception, the seven years is considered to begin with the breaking of the first seal in Revelation 6:1-2. However, it is possible to place the first four seals *prior to* the beginning of the seven years.

- The first indication the world will have of the potential identification of the Antichrist is the confirmation of a covenant with Israel (Dan. 9:26-27). However, it is possible that this could be done in secret or that there is more than one party to the confirmation.

  - This confirmation of the covenant is the event that starts the prophetic time-clock once again (seven years).

  - There is nothing Biblically that requires the confirmation of the covenant to be placed with the appearance of the Antichrist in the first seal (Rev. 6:1-2). That is, the covenant *could be* confirmed anywhere after the first seal and before the fifth seal.

Revelation 6:1-10: *The First Four Seals: The Four Horses of the Apocalypse*

Revelation 6:1-2: *The First Seal: The White Horse*

- In Revelation 1:2, we are told John wrote both *word* and *sight*. Here we begin to see why both were needed.

- The Greek word *phoneo* is the "noise" or "sound," often translated "voice" but not implying anything verbal, therefore **noise** is a better translation. Our English word *phonics* is "the science of sound." *Telephone* is "far away sound."

- The word "**bow**" is *toxon*, from which we get *toxic*, a word that developed due to the practice of putting poison on an arrow and shooting it from a bow to the enemy. This is unequivocally a weaponry word, verified in the fact that the rider goes **"forth conquering, and to conquer."**

- This is *stephanos*, the "victor's crown," which is a *perishable wreath*. The *diadema* is the royal crown, and is not used here.

- At this point, the rider begins his journey **conquering**, but has yet more to conquer.

- By assumption and inductive study, we believe this rider to be the Antichrist.

Revelation 6:3-4: *The second Seal: The Fiery Red Horse*

- The rider of this horse **take[s] peace** from the earth (that is, brings war).

- Verse 4 could be translated, "and in order that they would slay one another, also a great sword was given to him."

- The identity of this horseman is veiled. Is it also the Antichrist? Is it the false prophet? Is it simply the personification of warfare?
- The *result* and not the *identity of a person* is what is most important.

Revelation 6:5-6: *The Third Seal: The Black Horse*

- The rider of the black horse has **balances** *or scales* in his hands. In other passages, this word is translated *yoke*, and would also be a fitting translation here.
- The voice - Only the Critical Text makes this "as a voice" rather than "**a voice.**"
- Where is the voice coming from? "**In the midst**" not "in the center" (NASB) which sounds as if the voice was coming from the living creatures, which is possible but not verifiable.
- The price of wheat and barley has skyrocketed to exorbitant levels, indicating severe famine.
- There is a clear *prohibition* from harming the oil and wine.
  - Perhaps because oil and wine are used in worship, or perhaps because oil and wine are of the rich, who may be protected at this point.
  - There is no interpretive grid in scripture, so no definitive answer can be given.

Revelation 6:7-8: *The Fourth Seal: The Pale Horse*

- Come - Only the first four seals have the voice of the Living Creatures and the instruction, "**Come and see.**" This is a *very slight* indication that the first four seals are the *allowance or permission* for activity on earth, while what follows is the *direct work and will of God*.

- *Ashen* or **pale** is the Greek *chloros*, from which we get *chlorine*, *Clorox*, and *chloroform*.
- After this seal is broken, one-fourth of the earth is dead.

Revelation 6:9-11: *The Fifth Seal*

- The fifth seal is a period of proclamation and persecution.
    - It possibly covers the entire first 42 months of the Tribulation.
    - It almost certainly is in the first half of the Tribulation, ending with the Abomination of Desolation.
- **The Altar** (v. 9) - Recall that the Tabernacle was a shadow of the throne room of heaven, thus both have an altar. Since an altar is specifically for things *sacrificed*, we see here an altar of the *sacrifice of devotion*, not of atonement for sin.
- Verse 9 clearly tells the *reason* for the loss of life. However, it does not tell us the *timing* of the loss. Several possibilities arise, which should be investigated:
    - All martyrs of all time (this would imply no rapture had occurred)
    - All martyrs of the Christian era and of the era of the first four seals (this would also imply no rapture had occurred).
    - All martyrs of the post-rapture era (since the "dead in Christ" had already been raised).
- Verse 10 has echoes of Psalm 79:5-6, and several other "imprecatory" prayers.
    - It is not a characteristic cry of martyrs of the Age of Grace, who are to *refrain from prayers of vengeance* and **if thine enemy hunger, feed him** (Rom. 12:20).

- Note parallels with Luke 18:1-8.

▸ Verse 11 If **a little season** is said of the martyrs of all time or of the church age (see note on v. 9), then it seems inaccurate. The term *chronon micron* is a *micron of chronology*, which would only be true for those who die a martyr's death in the days after the rapture. The phrase can be interpreted using John 7:33, John 12:35, and Revelation 20:3.

Revelation 6:12-17: *The Sixth Seal*

The Day of the Lord's Wrath

▸ The sixth seal is so clear that it serves as a great test of interpretation. Use it when making judgments on commentary and teaching on the book of Revelation.

▸ Timing issues based on a comparison with Matthew 24:

- The seals make an almost unmistakable alignment with Matthew 24.
- The fifth seal corresponds to Matthew 24:9-28.
- The Abomination of Desolation is in Matthew 24:15 and is noted as the midpoint of the Tribulation in Daniel 9:27.
- Matthew 24:29-30 unarguably describes the same as the sixth seal of Revelation 6:12-17.
- Both Matthew 24 chronology and practical considerations would force the sixth seal somewhere after the midpoint of the tribulation.

▸ As with the other seals, there is a command to "behold." In this case, it is translated in KJV as "**lo**."

Revelation 6:12-15: *The Physical Nature of the Sixth Seal*

- A *seismos megas* is more than a **great earthquake.**
- Its effects are both in the heavens (sky) and on the earth.
- Effects in the heavens:
  - **The sun became black as sackcloth of hair.**
  - **The moon became as blood.**
  - Stars fall on the earth.
  - **The heaven departed**. Compare to Acts 15:39
- Effects on the earth:
  - Every mountain and island was moved
  - Men of all social and economic levels hid themselves, longing for death.
- The description of these events is so clear that any spiritualized interpretation must be disregarded in utter rejection if words have any meaning whatsoever.
  - This passage has had wild interpretations, from the conversion of Constantine to the French Revolution.

Revelation 6:16-17: *The Knowledge of the Men of Earth*

- They know that this is from **Him that sitteth on the throne**.
- They know that this is **the wrath of the Lamb.**
- They know that they cannot survive.
- Comparative Passages:
  - Haggai 2:6-7, 21-22
  - Joel 2:10-11, 30-31

Revelation 7:1-8: *The Sealing of the 144,000*

- Verses 1-8 answer the question of Revelation 6:17.

- In verse 1, **"after these things"** does not necessarily imply a direct chronology with the preceding seal. In fact, such chronology would be impossible. Rather, John says, in effect, "The next thing revealed to me was..."

- Note the repeated use of four. This is the number of "earthly" matters.

- The fact that there is no wind (v. 1) almost certainly places this before the sixth seal.

- Verses 2-3 – an angel with **the seal of the living God** prohibited the four angels from harming the earth, sea, or trees until the servants of God had been sealed.

- This effect of the sealing of the elect is culminated in Matthew 24:31. When Matthew 24:31 and Revelation 7:1-8 are connected, it is easy to see that the **elect** of whom Jesus spoke are completely of Israel.

- Of the 144,000: If this number is not literal, then no number in the book can be taken literally. Everything that follows is of a literal nature. There is no "figure of speech" discernable at all. Note that this definite number is contrasted to an indefinite number in verse 9. If the author wanted to express something vague, he clearly had the means to do so.

  - Daniel 12:1 shows that this number is a fixed and definite number.

- This 144,000 is the **nation** of Matthew 21:43.

- The tribes of Dan and Ephraim are missing from the list, substituting Levi and Joseph. The reason can be discerned from Deuteronomy

29:18-21. Dan and Ephraim were the first to introduce idolatry into Israel.

▶ How safe are the 144,000? They are as safe as the 12,000 of Numbers 31, especially verses 48-49.

Revelation 7:9-17: *The Innumerable Multitude*

Revelation 7:9-12: *The Scene in Heaven*

▶ Verse 9: As in Revelation 7:1, the phrase "**After this**" does not necessitate chronological order. In all likelihood, the outcome of verses 9-17 takes place over at least the first half of the tribulation, if not the entire seven years.

▶ Verse 9, **which no man could number,** - From *arithmos*, from which we get *arithmetic*. This is a very precise term, but was beyond ability to carry out with precision.

▶ Verse 9, **of all nations** -

- Though this is true of the church, it is not words the Scripture would use to describe the church.
- Theologically, the church is distinct from both Jew and Gentile, as a "new man," an entity unto itself.
- This multitude is gentile, distinct from both the 12 tribes and the church.
- Though this group is in heaven, that does not require that they be part of "the church." See verse 14 for their identity.

▶ Verse 9, **clothed with white robes** -

- White garments are mentioned several times in Revelation:

- They were promised to those in Sardis who overcome (Rev. 3:4-5)
- The Laodiceans were encouraged to purchase them (Rev. 3:18)
- The 24 Elders wore them (Rev. 4:4)
- The martyrs of the 5th seal wore them (Rev. 6:11)
- The martyrs of this passage wear them (Rev. 7:9, 13)
- The armies of heaven wear them upon the return of Jesus as King (Rev. 19:8, 14)
  - A significant grammatical detail concerning the white garments:
    - The preparation or purchase of the garments is always in the *active* tense (seen clearly in Rev. 19:8).
    - The presentation of the garments is always in the *passive* tense ("they were clothed," never "they clothed themselves.")
    - Because of the active tense of preparing the clothing, I do not see that anyone presented in the white garment in the book of Revelation is part of the church, including those of Revelation 19.
- Verse 9, **palms in their hands**, As on the day of the Triumphal entry, with a very similar cry.
- Verse 10, should say, "they are crying," rather than **"cried"** (KJV) or "cry" (NASB). John is describing what is taking place at the moment he is watching.

Revelation 7:13: *The Important Question from the Elder*

- The phrase "**answered, saying,**" or the similar phrase, "answered and said," is used when a literal question has not been asked, but an analysis of the situation is being given. The Greek *apokrinomai* is literally, "from a judgment (opinion)."

- If one of the Elders found the identity of this group to be important enough to ask the question, we should find it important to know the answer!

Revelation 7:14: *The Answer from the Elder*

- Because these **"came out of great tribulation"** or "out of the great tribulation" (NASB) they must have been in the great tribulation.

- It is important to note that, while the source of cleansing is the same (the blood of the Lamb), the method of cleansing has changed drastically from the Church Age. This helps answer the question, **"What are these which are arrayed in white robes? and whence came they?"** in verse 13. The active form of **washed** and **made** are incompatible with the age of Grace. Compare to Ephesians 2:8-9.

Revelation 7:15-17: *The Activity of The Multitude*

- Verse 15, "**Therefore**," is literally, "through this," and builds upon the washing of the garments in verse 14.

- Verse 15, **They serve him day and night…** - This is a vision in heaven. The Tabernacle was built on a model of Heaven; thus we have a glimpse of its shape and beauty. The New Heaven will have no "day and night" nor will it have a Temple, so this, like the earthly tabernacle, is temporary.

- Verse 15, To "tabernacle" among is to **dwell**.
  - When Peter saw the glory of the Lord at the Mt. of Transfiguration, he wanted to build a "tabernacle," not a church, synagogue, temple, or building.

- The Tabernacle and its feast were always future oriented, looking toward the time when God would dwell among His people.
- Verses 16-17 - Note that even when these are in Heaven during the days of the Tribulation, the promises are not delivered and the joy is not complete. The eschatology that doesn't include an earthly, physical kingdom is an unbiblical and incomplete eschatology.

Revelation 8:1-5: *The Seventh Seal*

Revelation 8:1-5: *The Introduction*

- The seventh seal is a continuous flow when it begins.
  - The breaking of the seal leads to the seven trumpets.
  - The seventh trumpet leads to the seven vials.
- The pattern of the seventh trumpet matches the pattern of the seven seals.
  - The first six seals take place on earth, the seventh in heaven.
    - The first six trumpets take place on earth, the seventh in heaven.
  - The first four seals are delivered with few words
    - The first four trumpets are delivered with few words
  - The final three seals are delivered with many words
    - The final three trumpets are delivered with over 50 verses.
- As in all the seals, the Lamb broke the seal (v. 1)
  - Note that "the Lamb" is implied in NASB, but the Greek simply says "he."

- The half-hour silence: The translation "**about**" is from the word for "as" or "like," thus the half-hour need not be exact, but there is also no reason to take it figuratively (for what would it figure?).
- The **seven trumpets** (v. 2) - There is no need to equate these with the **trump of God** (1 Thess. 4:16) or the "**last trump**" (1 Cor. 15:52). These are seven trumpets of angels.
- The censer and the incense (vv. 3-4)
  - The word for frankincense is *lambanos*. the utensil upon which it was burned is the *lambanotos*, or the **censer**.
  - The *lambanatos* was used in the Temple, on the Table of Shewbread and was **an offering made by fire, of a sweet savour unto the Lord** (Lev. 1:9).
  - The censer is simply the tool to carry the incense.
  - The incense, in this case, was added to the golden alter. In the Tabernacle, the golden altar was before the veil; here it is before the throne. This incense was added to the earlier incense that represented the prayers of the saints (Rev. 5:8).
  - The incense of worship added to the prayers is only a prelude to the seven trumpets.
- The judgment of the fire (v. 5)
  - Now the pause that began in Revelation 7:1-3 is lifted, and judgment begins again, and is about to come with vengeance.
  - The prayer of the saints and the judgment that comes when those prayers are answered is given prophetically is Psalm 18:4ff.

REVELATION 8:6–9:21:
THE SEVEN TRUMPETS

- As the first four trumpets blow, they will be in rapid-fire order, with no pause in-between.
- The textual separation between the sixth and seventh trumpet found in Revelation 10:1-11:14, is a parenthetical statement, not a pause in activity.

Revelation 8:7: *The First Trumpet*

- Hail, fire, and blood - Both here and in verse 8, there is no reason not to take this literally, including the blood.
  - Note that in Revelation 11:6 the two witnesses have the power to turn water to blood, and in the plagues of Egypt the Nile turned to blood.
  - "If the plain sense makes common sense, seek no other sense."
- There is no reason to question this as literal, yet the non-literal interpretations abound.
  - This first plague destroys a large part of the vegetation of the land of Israel. We see some fulfillment in this from Josephus... This is not a literal **hail (8:7)**. It is a symbolic one, one using

a symbol that cannot fail to picture the judgment that God, through the Romans, will now bring on the land. Bass, Ralph E. *Back to the Future: A Study in the Book of Revelation*. Greenville, SC: Living Hope Press, 2004. Print.

- These things may happen literally. We should, though, remain open to seeing a spiritual side of these happenings. They may occur literally and then spiritually or in concert with one another. Because of this, we will explore the spiritual potential for each of the trumpets where applicable... Spiritually, this first trumpet may refer to the trial by fire to which "every man's works" must be subjected (1 Corinthians 3:13–15). The works of every man will be tried by the "fire" of the Spirit of God, who knows every man's heart. If the works are built on Jesus, they will remain. If they are built on anything else, they will be destroyed by the "consuming fire" (Hebrews 12:29) of God. Fogle, Larry W. *Revelation Explained*. South Plainfield, NJ: Bridge Publishing, 1981. Print.

- The first angel sounded the first trumpet, and there followed hail and fire mingled with blood. A storm of heresies, a mixture of dreadful errors falling on the church, or a tempest of destruction. Henry, Matthew, and Thomas Scott. *Matthew Henry's Concise Commentary*. Oak Harbor, WA: Logos Research Systems, 1997. Print.

- By *blood* "we must naturally understand," says Professor Stuart, "in this case, a shower of coloured rain; that is, rain of a rubidinous aspect, an occurrence which is known sometimes to take place, and which, like falling stars, eclipses, &c., was viewed with terror by the ancients, because it was supposed to be indicative of blood that was to be shed." Barnes, Albert. *Notes on the New Testament: Revelation*. Ed. Robert Frew. London: Blackie & Son, 1884–1885. Print.

- The symbols in vision next following were such as well to suit those Gothic devastations,—being the symbols of thunderings, lightnings, and an earthquake, then, after trumpet-soundings from on high, those of tempests, volcanoes, and meteors, successively bursting on the Roman earth,—it seems to me almost impossible to doubt but that the latter were intended as a prefiguration of the former. Elliott, E. B. *Horæ Apocalypticæ; Or, A Commentary on the Apocalypse, Critical and Historical.* Fifth Edition. Vol. 1. London: Seeley, Jackson, and Halliday, 1862. Print.

Revelation 8:8-9: *The Second Trumpet*

▸ **as it were a great mountain (v. 8)** - John consistently makes the reader aware when he is using analogy rather than literal terms. The Greek term *os* "as" or "like" is used 65 times in Revelation.

▸ A third of the sea became blood - If Exodus 8:20 and Psalm 78:44 are literal, why not this?

Revelation 8:10-11: *The Third Trumpet*

▸ Wormwood - There is really no way to interpret "Wormwood."
  - Clearly the result is that the waters were "bitter," but *bitter* is not the translation of *apsinthos*.
  - The Hebrew equivalent is used eight times in the Old Testament, always with a judgment connotation.
  - Whatever it is, it causes death from the waters.

▸ An interpretation is not needed, the results speak for themselves.

Revelation 8:12-13: *The Fourth Trumpet*

- Just like the fourth seal took place in heaven, the fourth trumpet affects "the heavens."

- The fourth trumpet is simply an announcement and warning of woe.

- It is by an **angel** or "eagle" (modern translations), due to a textual variant. Angel seems to fit best in context and in connection with Revelation 14:6 and even Revelation 19:17.

Revelation 8:13: *The Triple Woe*

- "Midheaven" (NASB) or **midst of heaven** is the zenith – the highest point in the sky, where the sun shines at noon.

- The final three trumpets are also the three "woes."

Revelation 9:1-12: *The Fifth Trumpet*

- Verse 1 – **Fifth** - A Greek tip: any Greek word that ends in "*-tos*" can be translated "that which is [root word]."

  - Here, *pemtos* is built on the root word *pente* (meaning "five"), so *pentos* is "that which is five."

  - The *-tos* suffix is common and an understanding of its meaning is helpful.

- Verse 1 – the fallen star:

  - In Revelation, interpret everything literally unless the literal translation makes no sense. A star fallen to earth makes sense literally, until you see that it is given a key, and this "star" opens the pit. It only makes sense, therefore, to see this star as representative of someone.

- Using good rules of interpretation (Namely, "Scripture interprets Scripture"), one must determine the meaning of the representation.
  - "Hosts of heaven" are both stars (Deut. 4:19) and angels (1 Kings 22:19).
  - In Revelation 8:10, it makes sense to see the star as a literal star.
  - In Revelation 1:20, seven stars are clearly seven people.
  - In Revelation 9:11, it is possible that this **king over them** is also the fallen star.
  - In Luke 10:18, Jesus speaks of seeing Satan **fall from heaven**, using the same words as verse 1.
  - In Revelation 12:9 Satan falls from heaven.
  - In Isaiah 14:12-19 Lucifer falls from heaven.
- While it cannot be determined exclusively, it looks like this "star" is Satan himself.

▶ Verse 1 – **the key** – Whether literal or figurative matters not. The key clearly opened the pit. There is no need to create a symbolism.

▶ Verse 1 – **the bottomless pit** –

- "Bottomless" is *abussos*, which is *a-* (the negator) and *buthos* (a deep pool of water, even the ocean). It is literally, "without depth."
  - The word is often not translated, but left as "abyss," as in Luke 8:31 or Romans 10:7 (NASB).
  - It is the home of **the beast** in Revelation 17:8, and the place

where Satan is imprisoned by an angel, who is given the key, in Revelation 20:1-3.
- The abyss is *not* hell, but is a place of imprisonment for demonic forces.
  - Which demonic forces are being released at this time? It is not known, but the Abyss is likely the same place where **angels which kept not their first estate** and are now in **everlasting chains under darkness** (Jude 1:6).

▸ Verse 3 – the **locusts** – It cannot be doubted that these are locusts nor that these locusts are more accurately demons that had been imprisoned. They are, therefore, "possessed locusts," with an unusual appearance, seen in verse 7.

▸ Verse 4 – the vegetation - These possessed locusts with Scorpion-like power have instruction to avoid doing that which locusts would typically do: eat vegetation. Rather, they were to harm a specific group of men. This displays the authority of heaven over all demonic power.

▸ Verse 5 – **torment** - from *basanos*. The *basalt* stone was used to reveal the true quality of gold. The word *basanos* and *basalt* came to be associated with torture because the scraping of the gold "brought out the truth" about its quality. To be tortured is to be scraped against the stone until the truth is revealed.

▸ Verse 11 – **Abaddon** - The Hebrew word is used six times in the Hebrew Scriptures, referring to the destroyer (though often translated as the place of the dead, synonymous with Sheol).

Revelation 9:13-21: *The Sixth Trumpet*

- Verse 13 – **the golden altar** - This is the golden altar of incense, described in Exodus 30:3 and following. See Revelation 8:3 also.
- Verses 14-15 – **the four angels** - These could be good or evil "angels," but appear to be demonic.
  - Verse 14 is evidence that angels have assignments that are very specific in duty as well as timing.
  - Clearly, God knows exactly when this event will take place.
  - It is not appropriate to build a theology for "all times, places, and circumstances" based on the precision of this verse.
    - We do not know if all angels at all times and in all places have such a prepared and structured role.
    - It is possible that in the Age of Grace, God has allowed a free will that is unprecedented in human history.
- Verse 16 – **the army of the horsemen** –
  - Presumably, this army is controlled by the four angels of verse 15.
  - There is no reason to consider these horsemen as symbolic of some human army or otherwise, especially considering their description in verse 17. They are simply the horsemen of the four angels, presumably of a spiritual nature themselves.
  - While a "myriad" is sometimes just "countless," this number is too specific to be called countless. First, there are "two myriads of myriads." Second, John "heard the number of them." When used literally, a myriad is 10,000.
- Verses 20-21 – **The rest of the men…repented not**. This is indication that the age of Grace has ceased (Grace not being an age

of repentance of works), and that the delusion promised by Paul has arrived.

- Revelation 10:1-11:14 continue as part of the 2nd woe (which is the 6th trumpet).

REVELATION 10:1-11:19:
A PARENTHETICAL STATEMENT

Revelation 10:1-11: *A Strong Messenger With a Message*

Revelation 10:1-2: *The Mighty Angel*

▸ The Angel's Description:

- While the description of this angel sounds like Christ, the designation as **another mighty angel** needs to be taken literally.

- A strong angel is seen in Revelation 5:2, asking, **"Who is worthy...?"** That strong angel was clearly not Christ.

- The description alone cannot be used to override the words chosen and inspired.

- Verses 5-6 are problematic if Christ is the angel of verses 1-2.

- If Christ is not the angel, who is it? It is simply best to not go further than what John reveals: it is another strong angel. The Christ-like description of the angel does not require that the angel be Christ.

- The angel stood on land and sea.
    - This fact is noted three times (v. 2, 5, 8), and must have significance.
    - It is likely an image of dominion.
    - Whereas the judgment has been described beginning in chapter 5 with the "big book," the judgment is going to be completed with the contents of this little book.
    - This angel comes to take a position of strength, dominion, and conquest of sea and land.
- The Angel's Possession:
    - This little book is not defined, but is clearly a book that reveals further judgment. More of its content is seen in following verses.

Revelation 10:3-7: *The Mighty Message*

- The voice (v. 3):
    - Unlike John's cry of chapter 5, this is not a cry of sadness. This is a display of power.
- The seven thunders (v. 3-4):
    - The Greek includes a definite article, **the seven thunders**. These thunders are given personification with **voices**.
- The instruction (v. 4):
    - The things spoken were known by John but are not known to us. They are a "mystery" in the Biblical sense. Since they are unknown, speculation is unfruitful.
    - When John wrote, it was to reveal. He was told not to write in order to conceal.

- o Many students want to take what John wrote and treat it as if it is concealed, and then want to take what John didn't write and want to reveal.
- o John's writing was so clear that the voice from heaven did not want him to write, but rather wanted it to remain known only to John.

▸ The identification clue (verses 5-6):

- These verses make an interpretation of the mighty angel as Christ to be problematic.
- Christ is the creator of all things (Col. 1:16, Jn. 1:3), and therefore cannot also be the mighty angel.

▸ The message itself (vv. 6-7):

- Time itself will not cease to exist (as seen in Rev. 20), but rather "time to judgment" is about to be completed.
- The prayer of the Martyrs ("how long…") is about to be answered.
- When the 7th trumpet sounds (v. 7), **time** is up.
- It would be a terrible theological flaw to conclude that the **mystery of God** in this verse is the same as the mystery revealed to the Apostle Paul.
  - o The mystery of the church revealed to Paul was unknown before Paul (Eph. 3:9)
  - o The mystery of the church is called the **mystery of Christ** (Eph. 3:4) and was revealed to Paul by Christ, directly.
  - o This **mystery of God** was **declared to his servants the prophets** by God.
  - o Whatever this mystery is, we should be able to find in the Hebrew Scriptures, revealed through the prophets.

- Note: be careful when allowing Scripture to interpret Scripture that you do it faithfully, not sloppily. If the **mystery** here were the church, then the church would be in the tribulation. There is no need to go with this, however, when we also see **mystery** used outside the church, as in Matthew 13:10, 11, 34, 35.
- Note also: the phrase **"his servants the prophets"** is used 7 times, always in the Old Testament except this case.
- There are similarities between John's experience and that of Daniel in Daniel 12, especially since the 1,260 days is both in Daniel 12 and Revelation 11:2-3.

Revelation 10:8-11: *The Sweet and Sour Book*

▶ The request (v. 8-9): Take and eat the book.

▶ The result (vv. 9-10):
- Compare Ezekiel 2:8-3:7.
- There is a sweetness to knowing that "the time has come." There is bitterness to pronouncing judgment on Israel.

▶ The repetition (v. 11):
- "**Again**" is likely not a reference to John's previous prophecies, but rather the prophecies given to the prophets in verse 7 must be proclaimed again.
- The Greek word *epi* is literally "upon." A good English interpretation would be "against."

Revelation 11:1-13: *The Two Witnesses*

Revelation 11:1-2: *The Times of the Gentiles*

- ▸ Do not fail to connect Revelation 11:1 with 10:11. This is a continuation of the scene of chapter 10. The measurement is part of the prophecy of Revelation 10:11.

- ▸ The Measurement of the Temple

  - The word was used of a reed that, depending on size, was used for a number of purposes.
    - The smallest were filled with ink and made into pens, thus the word can, in context, mean pen.
    - The size variation is the reason John clarifies that this reed is **like unto a rod**.
    - The English word "calamari" comes from *calamus*, because types of calamari are hollow and contain natural ink.

  - We would first expect this to be the Temple in heaven. However, the information of verse 2 forces us to consider this to be a future, Tribulation-era Temple.
    - The fact that this Tribulation-era Temple is called, **"of God"** gives indication that the Tribulation temple could be the Millennial Temple.
    - 2 Thessalonians 2:1-4 also refers to the **"temple of God"** in reference to the Tribulation Temple.
    - The New Jerusalem, after the millennium, will not have a Temple (Rev. 21:22).
    - More likely, however, the Millennial Temple will be built by Christ Himself, after His return, and will match the description of Ezekiel 40-45. See Zechariah 6:13.

- The Meaning of the measurement
  - The measurements are never actually given.
  - The meaning of the measurements must be in the allotment of time in which **the holy city** is given to the gentiles.
    - The city is eternally holy, regardless of the events taking place within its gates.
  - The time-period is 42 months.
    - One-half of the Tribulation period. My interpretation is that the reference is to the last half of the Tribulation. (1,260 days, v. 3)
    - Other passages that refer to a **"times of the Gentiles"** - Luke 21:24, Romans 11:25.

Revelation 11:3-12: *The Two Witnesses*

- Because these are presented as a "known fact," the student of the Word should search the Scriptures for information.
  - Zechariah 4:11-14 is the only other mention (with the assumption that they are the same).
  - Note the reference to two olive trees in verse 4, which make a strong case that these witnesses match that of Zechariah.
- Their purpose:
  - Stand before the God of the earth (v. 4)
  - Destroy their enemies (v. 5)
    - **if any man will hurt them** –
      - The Greek *adikeo* is the opposite of *dike*, which is justice.

- ✓ If someone studies theodicy (*theo dike*), they are studying the "justness of God."
    - ◆ Therefore, "if anyone treats them unjustly" is a good interpretation.
  - ○ Fire out of their mouth. Compare 2 Kings 1:10-12.
- Control judgments upon the earth (v. 6)
  - ○ While the identity of the two witnesses is mere speculation, this verse has led many to ponder whether Elijah and Moses are in view.
  - ○ Elijah shut up the rains for 3 1/2 years (Jas. 5:17; Lk. 4:25)
  - ○ Moses turned the waters to blood and smote the earth with plagues.

▶ Their pain:

- Their purpose comes to an end when they **have finished their testimony**, (v. 7).
- They are then killed by the beast (v. 7) -
  - ○ Because the beast does not ascend out of the bottomless pit until Revelation 17, where is given authority for **one hour** (Rev. 17:12), when he will then **make war** with the Lamb and His followers (Rev. 19:19), this verse must be a foreshadow of that which is to later occur, at the end of the 42 months.
- Their bodies are mocked (vv. 8-9) -
  - ○ Their bodies lie in the streets of Jerusalem
    - ◆ Verse 8 is yet another great example of how John writes clearly, not in obscurity.
      - ✓ If he has figurative language, he always defines it.

- - ✓ In Isaiah 1, Israel is referred to, figuratively, as Sodom, and as Egypt in Ezekiel 23.
  - A burial is not allowed (v. 9) –
    - Failure to bury a criminal put to death brings a curse upon the land, according to Deuteronomy 21:22-23.
    - Jewish teaching: *"It is considered a matter of great shame and discourtesy to leave the deceased unburied--his soul has returned to God, but his body is left to linger in the land of the living. Even a Priest, on his way to enter the sanctuary on Yom Kippur, was commanded to render this honor of immediate burial even to a strange corpse, although he is normally forbidden to handle the remains. This is the proper honor that Jewish tradition accords those who die."* (http://www.chabad.org/library/article_cdo/aid/281551/jewish/Timing-the-Funeral-Service.htm)
  - The people of the earth celebrate their death, until they are resurrected and raptured (vv. 10-12).
    - Their rapture (v. 12) is unlike the rapture, which is **in the twinkling of an eye** (1 Cor. 15:52).

Revelation 11:13-14: *The Completion of the Second Woe*

- These are the two witnesses of the second woe.
  - The woe begins in Revelation 9:13, is interrupted in Revelation 10:1, and picks up in Revelation 11:13.
- The second woe concludes with a great earthquake.
  - This also helps us with timing, since there is a great earthquake in Revelation 16:18-19, which is at the conclusion of the Battle of Armageddon.

- 7,000 men are slain in the earthquake.
- The rest or the remnant?
    - **Remnant** (v. 13) is more literally translated "the rest/remainder," as in Revelation 19:21.
    - However, the timing would be appropriate for a mass conversion of Jews, and thus **remnant** *could be* a valid interpretation, but not solidly verifiable.
    - In Revelation 19:7, there is a multitude that gives God glory **because his wife hath made herself ready**. Is this a foreshadow of that remnant?
    - The challenge to this is that the Greek uses a different word for the remnant of Israel.

Revelation 11:15-19: *The Seventh Trumpet*

Revelation 11:15-17: *The Forecast of Reign*

▶ The **angel sounded** (v. 15) - Literally, "sounded his trumpet." The Greek word is only used of trumpets.

▶ The kingdoms of the world –

- This should be plural (as in KJV) and not singular (as in NASB).
- **"Are become"** is an antiquated form of "have become."
- When does this take place?
    - Today, they are still "of this world," ruled by the "god of this age."
    - A claim that says this has already happened in the current age does not align with Scripture.

- All of verses 15-19 is a forecast and early celebration of what is yet to come.
  - **He shall reign** - Note that by the seventh trumpet the kingdoms become the Lord's, but the reign is *yet future*.
- **The Lord God Almighty** – (v. 17)
  - The Greek word *"pantokrator"* comes from two roots, *pas (pan)* = "all" and *kratos* = power.
  - Many English "power" words include the root *kratos*, including democracy and autocracy.
- **Thou hast taken…and hast reigned** – (v. 17)
  - **"Thou hast taken"** is a perfect active indicative verb.
    - Indicative is a statement of fact
    - Active means the work was done by the subject (God)
    - Perfect means that it happened at a point in time and yet the effect continues to the present.
  - **"Hast reigned"** is an aorist active indicative verb.
    - The "active indicative" are as above.
    - However, rather than "perfect" tense, the aorist tense implies something that happens in a singular point in time, whether past, present, or future.
    - Therefore, **this verb does not indicate that the Lord is reigning at the moment of this speech.**
      - Note that in verse 15 the reign is future.
      - In Greek, to speak of a yet future event in the aorist is not uncommon, yet is notoriously difficult to translate to English, which only has past, present,

or future tenses.

- For examples of the aorist used in the future, see Matthew 18:15 and Hebrews 2:8 (which has the same subject matter as Rev. 11:15-17--the future reign).

- Note that NASB incorrectly translates "**hast reigned**" into a perfect rather than an aorist. The same is true of ESV, NIV, HCSB, TEV, and many others.

  - Taking this liberty without explanation as to why it should not be done in the other aorist active verbs is inexcusable.
  - For example, the verb "**is come**" in verse 18 is in the same tense as "**hast reigned**" in verse 17.
  - If the reign has begun, the wrath has also begun, but the translators of modern versions have allowed reign without wrath.

- The major theological point: at the sound of the seventh trumpet God has taken power, but He will not begin His reign until He sends His Son to re-establish David's throne (fulfilling the question and desire of Acts 1:6).

- In practical matters, this makes important worldview differences and an entire system of charismatic and neocharismatic theology has arisen because of an "inaugurated eschatology" in which Christ reigns in heaven before His wrath is poured on earth and His Davidic throne is established.

Revelation 11:18-19: *The Response on Earth and Heaven*

▸ The nations were angry (v. 18) - This is the fulfillment of Psalm 2:1 and 110:5.

▸ **The time of the dead** (v.18) –

- This **time of the dead** must be the resurrection of the dead, but specifically the first resurrection of Revelation 20, which takes place at the second coming.
- It is the first because it is the giving of rewards (the *and* should be taken as a connection between judgment and rewards). At the second resurrection, there are no rewards, only punishment.

▸ Those involved at the first resurrection (v. 18)-

- This phrase tells us who is involved in this resurrection, namely three groups:
  - God's servants the prophets (Old Testament era).
  - The saints (Jewish believers from the call of Abraham to the end of the Kingdom offer)- "the holy ones."
  - Those who **fear thy name**-- dead believers of the Tribulation era.
- Notice that the "dead in Christ" (i.e.: those of the church age) are not included, since they have been previously resurrected.

▸ God will **destroy them which destroy the earth** (V. 18)—

- Any eschatology which does not have a place for the restoration of the earth is an unbiblical eschatology (i.e.: amillennialism).

▸ The opening of the Temple of heaven (v. 19)—

- Much of this remains a mystery.
- The earthly Temple, along with its contents, is only a shadow of the heavenly temple, including the ark.
- In my estimation, this is the ark of "His covenant," likely the new covenant of Jeremiah 31, and not to be equated with the Ark of the Covenant in the Tabernacle (which was a shadow of the Ark of His Covenant in Heaven).

- Lightening, voices, thundering, an earthquake, great hail (v. 19)—
  - This takes place on earth at the close of the seventh trumpet.

REVELATION 12-15:
BEHIND THE SCENES

- The book of Revelation is not chronological, and proper interpretation requires placing one passage upon another. There are parenthetical statements throughout the book.
- Revelation 6:1-17 begins the chronology of the Tribulation
- Revelation 7 is laid on top of Revelation 6.
- Revelation 8-9 continue where Revelation 6 left off.
- Revelation 10:1-11:14 is laid on top of Revelation 8-9.
- Revelation 11:15-19 continues where Revelation 9 left off.
- Revelation 12-15 are laid upon the chronological Revelation of 6, 8-9, and 11:15-19.
- Each of the parenthetical passages describes behind the scenes information about the explicit chapters.
- Revelation 16-22 continue where Revelation 11:19 stops.

Revelation 12:1-17: *The Sign and the War in Heaven*

Revelation 12:1-2: *The Woman*

- **A great wonder** -- More literally, a sign.

  - The word carries the inherent meaning of providing information.
  - This also tells us, clearly, that what is about to happen is not literal, but rather provides information that we should know.

- **Clothed with the sun** -- Literally, "cast round about with the sun." The word is used of the lilies of the field that are **arrayed** (Lk. 12:27), and can also mean "clothed" in a literal sense.

- Who is this woman?

  - Beware of eisegesis, and allow Scripture to interpret Scripture.
  - There is zero evidence that this woman is Mary (as per Catholic interpretation).
    - Genesis 37:9-10 show Jacob as the "sun," Rachel as the "moon," and the brothers as the "stars." This image is so similar that it would be irresponsible not to include this in the interpretation. Thus, the image appears to be that of the totality of Israel--the patriarchs, matriarchs, and tribes.
    - Zechariah 9:16 speaks of the tribes of Israel as **stones of a crown.**
  - When all analysis is done, it is almost impossible to view this *woman* as anything other than the nation of Israel.
  - The Papal church has depicted the virgin Mary as this woman because they are unable to concede that Israel has a permanent, future, Kingdom role. Rather, they see themselves as the

Kingdom (thus as Israel).

- Protestant churches are equally guilty at incorrect depictions of the woman, often describing her as "the people of God" or "the church."

▸ Israel **pained to be delivered** (v.2)

- Literally, "Travailing in pain and being tortured to give birth, she, being with child [her Messiah], cried."

- This verse describes the painful longing of Israel for her Messiah. It is expressed well in the hymn "O Come O Come Immanuel."

Revelation 12:3-4: *Satan*

▸ Both the Dragon (Satan) and the Beast (the Antichrist) are depicted as having seven heads and ten horns. Since the Antichrist is the "son" of the devil, this is no surprise.

- There were seven Kingdoms that attempted to annihilate the Jewish people: Egypt, Syria, Assyria, Babylon, Persia, Greece, and Rome.

- While it cannot be definitively determined from Scripture that this is the meaning of the seven heads, it is a likely candidate for interpretation.

▸ The ten horns are the horns of the final empire, Rome (Dan. 7:7).

▸ The last four of the **heads** is depicted in the final four empires, and the last of the empire is made up of 10 kings (who give their power to the beast). The beast's empire composes the entire territory of the four Kingdoms (and almost certainly more).

▸ The **stars of heaven** are not to be confused with the stars of verse 1. These stars are angels, who become demons.

- Satan **drew** one-third of the angels (stars of heaven) - This is a more violent word than "draw," as other usages in the New Testament make clear. "Drag" would be more accurate.

- The desire to devour -- This verse explains 100% of antisemitism. It also is the interpretive key to...

  - the necessity of the flood
  - the difficulty of conception for Abraham and Sarah
  - the hatred of Ishmael and Esau toward Isaac, Jacob, and their descendants
  - the edicts of Pharaoh
  - the wilderness rebellions
  - the marriages of Solomon
  - the slaughter of the innocents under Herod

Revelation 12:5: *The Child*

- The man **who was to rule** –The verb *mello* is "to be on the point of doing something." So, more literally, "He is about to rule..."

- The child **was caught up**— This is a picture of the ascension.

  - Note that He is caught up to God and to God's throne...not to the throne of David.
  - Note the poor translation of "The Message," which places Christ on his own throne.

Revelation 12:6: *The Woman, Revisited*

- The church age is between verses 5 & 6, thus verse 6 and following are future.

- Those who reject a pre-tribulation rapture consistently interpret the woman here to be "the church," yet they do so without justification nor explanation.
- Compare Psalm 91 and the **secret place of the Most High**, which is a place of total protection. Psalm 91 is almost undoubtedly prophetic of this hiding place for Israel.
- **That they should feed her** -- Who is "they?"
  - Many translations change the clear use of third person plural active verb to a third person singular passive verb.
  - There is no excuse for this kind of outright fabrication of translation.
  - Could this be a reference to the "**I was an hungred, and ye gave me meat**" imagery of Matthew 25?
- 1,260 days - This is the last half of the Tribulation, after **them which be in Judaea flee** (Matt. 24:16). During this same time, the two witnesses are doing their work, and the 144,000 are sealed and proclaiming the gospel of the Kingdom.

Revelation 12:7-9: *The War in Heaven*

- **There was a war in heaven**
  - The tense of the verb does not necessitate past tense.
    - See the same usage in Matthew 7:28.
    - This tense is consistently used in Revelation for something that is, at the time of the writing, yet future (Rev. 6:12, 8:1, and, most closely in context, Rev. 12:10 "**now is come salvation...**").
  - The Greek word is *polemos*, from which we get "polemics," which is a verbal "battle."

- The Greek term is inclusive of all kinds of hostilities.
- *Polemos* is used three times in verse 7, here in noun form, and two times in verb form (translated, "**fought**.")

- Michael and His Angels (v. 7)
  - Michael is designated as the archangel in Jude 1:9.
  - The only other time we see him (except in this passage) is Daniel 10:13, 21, 12:1, where he is acting on behalf of the Jewish nation.

- **Fought against the dragon** - the dragon is prominent in chapter 12, and identified in Revelation 12:9 and 20:2.

- In verses 8-9 there is a threefold emphasis that Satan was cast out of heaven.
  - Since the Revelation is a future prophecy, this cannot be taken as a review of what happened at the fall of Lucifer.
  - Rather, the access Satan has before God *will be* removed.
  - Today Satan is the accuser of brethren, accusing them before God (v. 10). That day will come to an end!

- Notice that Satan, at the point of this casting out, is not cast into the abyss. He can still practice his deception on earth… and will.

Revelation 12:10-12a: *The Good Results of the War*

- The Proclamation of victory (v. 10) - Note that this proclamation is yet to occur in reality. The Kingdom has not come.

- **The accuser of our brethren** (v. 10) -
  - The Greek word *katagoros* is "accuser." From it we get "category" in English. Satan is scouring through every category to find

anything to use against the brethren.

- Note that though we almost always say, "the accuser of the brethren" it is literally, "**our brethren**," and a reference to the Jewish people.
  - Compare to Zechariah 3:1.
  - While this may be true of all Christians, Satan has always been more interested and concerned with the Jewish nation.

▶ **And they overcame him** (v. 11) -

- Don't make the mistake of removing the prophetic element from verse 11, making it something of the past.
- In the future, "the brethren" will overcome Satan by the blood, the word, and will sacrifice unto death.
- Prophetically, this verse speaks of the future remnant of Israel.
- For use of the same verb (overcame) used in the same form (Aorist/active/indicative) to refer to something yet future, see Revelation 5:5.

▶ **Therefore rejoice** (v. 12) -

- The Greek word *euphren* is based on *phren* (to understand) and the prefix *-eu*, (good).
- From *phren* we get schizophrenic and frantic.
- This is an imperative: have a good understanding of what has just occurred, put some thought into this, look at this correctly, and therefore REJOICE!

▶ **Ye that dwell** (v. 12) -

- Literally, "tabernacle in them."
- This particular word (σκηνουντες) is only used of heavenly beings and of Jesus who **dwelt among us** (Jn. 1:14).

Revelation 12:12b-16: *The Bad Results of the War*

- **Woe to the inhibitors of the earth** (v. 12-13) -

  - Notice that Satan does still have **a short time**.
  - This short time will be a time of Satan's wrath upon the Jews, his last-ditch effort to eradicate the "Jewish problem."
  - Satan's persecution of the woman who had the **man child** -
    - While KJV and NASB insert "child," the word simply implies "male" or "man."
    - In the context of the Jewish faith, "the Man" would be the Messiah.

- The woman flies to the wilderness (v. 14) -

  - Since the term **"eagles' wings"** is used of God's work in the days of the Exodus (Ex. 19:4), it is not necessary to see this as literal, but rather as protection from God.
  - Previously (v. 6) the woman *fled*, but now she is given ability to *fly*.
    - It appears that, as the woman was fleeing, Satan was cast out, and the woman needed supernatural ability to *fly*, lest she not make it to the place of refuge in time.
  - A NOTE ON TIMING:
    - Since she is there for **a time, and times, and half a time** (3 1/2 years), this war in heaven must take place at the midpoint of the tribulation.
    - When discerning Jews take heed of the words of Jesus about fleeing to the wilderness when the abomination of desolation occurs (Mt. 24:15-16), Satan comes into heaven to accuse the brethren, but Michael enters into battle and casts

him down to earth, where for 3 1/2 years he will savagely attack all Jews.
- It is also during this last half that the Two Witnesses will do their work.
- In the wilderness, the woman is nourished (v. 14) -
  - Notice the comparison with verse 6 **"they should feed her."**
  - Here, **"she is nourished"** is passive. It gives every appearance that *some group of gentiles* is feeding Israel. It is this group that will hear, **"Inasmuch as ye have done it unto one of the least of these my brethren, ye have done it unto me"** (Matt. 25:40).

▶ Satan sends **water as a flood** - (v. 15) -

- More literally, "as a river."
- The Greek word is *potamos* from which we get the Potomac River and words like *Mesopotamia* ("middle of two rivers"), and *hippopotamus* ("river horse").
- Satan does this so "that he might make her as one carried away by a river" (literal translation). This is the devil's hatred for Israel.

▶ The earth's assistance (v. 16) -

- The earth is at the Lord's command, so certainly God is behind the earth helping the woman.
- However, since the earth itself is under the curse, it has a perfect motive for helping the woman, through whom the curse will ultimately be lifted.

Revelation 12:17: *The Rest of the Jewish Nation*

- While not perfectly clear, it appears that this **remnant of her seed** is the portion of Israel that has not been carried to the hiding place of the wilderness.

    - Since, in the last day, God will **gather together his elect** from all corners of the globe (Matt. 24:31), the hiding place must be for only a portion of Israel.

- This **remnant** that is not in the hiding place is a specific group... they keep the commandments AND have the testimony of Jesus.

    - That is, they are believing Jews who are not living in the church (which is free from the Law), but are living in the remaining seven-year period of the Law that is, as of now, yet to come.

    - There seems to be a place of protection for the 144,000 (and possibly others) that is full and complete, in the wilderness, yet there are other Jews who will not be in that place. But, in the end, **all Israel shall be saved** (Rom. 11:26).

- This same remnant is mentioned in Revelation 14:12-13 as those who do not take the mark of the beast, therefore many of them **die in the Lord** prior to the second coming.

Revelation 13:1-2: *The Beast out of the Sea*

- Someone stood on the sands of the sea - verse 1

    - These words are included as Revelation 12:18 in some texts.

    - The Critical Text changes "I stood" to "he stood," referring to the dragon.

    - No doctrinal significance is evident. However, if it is the dragon standing on the sea, then the sea could be interpreted as in Revelation 17:15 as "the people's of the earth," thus, Satan was cast down to earth and stood on the shifting sands of earth's citizenry.

- ▶ The beast -
  - Just as John used the dragon figuratively as Satan, there is every reason to take this figuratively as the antichrist.
  - In context, this appears to happen at the midpoint of the Tribulation. The Antichrist has been on the scene for years, but not as the one-world ruler who establishes himself as god.
  - The seven heads likely represent the seven empires that attempted to annihilate the Jewish people: Egypt, Syria, Assyria, Babylon, Persia, Greece, and Rome.
    - This displays an important truth about the Antichrist: his sole agenda is to rid the earth of Jews.
  - The ten horns are the ten kings of the last-days Roman empire.
    - The ten horns are noted in Daniel 7, but only in Revelation do the horns have crowns.
    - By the fulfillment of this prophecy, the ten kings will be reigning monarchs.
  - The name of blasphemy -
    - The Greek word, βλασφημία (blasphamia) comes from βλάπτω (blapto) - «to hurt» and φήμη (pheme) «to declare your thoughts publicly.»
    - The Antichrist has no qualms about publicizing his hatred for God.
  - The likeness of the beast - (v. 2) -

- These are the same descriptions Daniel used in Daniel 7 to describe the kingdoms of Babylon, Persia, and Greece.
- Daniel then described a **"dreadful and terrible"** beast that was the fourth Kingdom, Rome.
- Notice, however, that John says that the beast was **"like unto,"** and was not the actual kingdoms. This is problematic for the preterist interpretation that claims the beast IS the Roman empire.

- The source of authority - (v. 2) - the devil.
  - Here, Satan gives all authority for earthly rule to the Antichrist, just as God did to His Son ("all authority is given to me....").
  - Today, the devil is the "god of this age," and he will give his authority to "satan incarnate," who is the Antichrist.

Revelation 13:3: *The Wounded Head*

- If the interpretation of the **heads** is correct (the seven empires that sought to destroy Israel), then "one of its heads" must be one of these nations.

- The most likely candidate, because it fits other prophecy, would be the empire of Rome, which took a fatal blow in the division of the empire, but prophecy says it will come together in a union of 10 kings, as one empire again.

- The world will both celebrate and be in awe of the revived Roman empire.

- There is no need to spiritualize the empire--it is a literal Roman empire based in Rome.

- Note: many prophecy teachers teach that the Antichrist will die and be resurrected, based on this verse. It is a position I previously held. However, when translating "heads" as "nations," such an interpretation is unmerited.

Revelation 13:4: *Future Worship*

- No matter how secular society becomes, it cannot get away from its need to worship.

- The Greek word is προσκυνέω (*proskuneo*) and literally means «toward (pros) a dog (kuon)» - that is, «to behave like a dog.» As odd as this seems, consider the love and loyalty of an obedient dog. This is the «model» for worship.

- Our world is looking for a hero, regardless of his connections.

- This verse refers to the beast as "him" (KJV). Literally, however, «it.» The Greek pronouns in reference to the beast are in the neuter form throughout the chapter.

- This leads one to ask, "Is the beast a HIM (person) or an IT (nation)?"

  - In a sense, both. The Antichrist is who he is because he is the *Caesar* of the new Rome.
  - But what is Caesar without the empire?
  - There are too many references to *personhood* to claim that the Antichrist is the empire.

Revelation 13:5-10: *The Blasphemous Reign*

- The *mouth* and the *power* must have been given by Satan, and permitted by God, the Supreme Authority.

- The forty-two months: this is the last half of the Tribulation. During this same time period, the following also takes place -
  - The two witnesses do their work,
  - The God-built shelter for a portion of the Jews is being used,
  - The devil is working through the Antichrist and other means to kill all Jews.
- The blasphemy spoken – verse 6
  - The name of God
  - The tabernacle of God -
    - This could be the Temple, but John typically uses the usual word for Temple (ναός - *naos*), as in Revelation 11:1.
    - I think it is more likely the hiding place in the wilderness, since *tabernacle* is the Greek word σκηνή (*skene*), which means «tent» or «dwelling place.»
    - The Antichrist (and the Dragon) are incensed that they cannot get to the Jews, hidden in God's *tabernacle* in the wilderness.
  - Those who dwell in heaven -
    - Literally, "them that *tabernacle* in heaven."
    - There are Jews in the hidden tabernacle and Jews, now dead, tabernacling in Heaven.
    - The Antichrist hates them even after they are dead, and continues to blaspheme them.
- The reign of terror - verse 7
  - Satan *offered* the kingdoms of the world to the Messiah, but He would not take them. The Antichrist will take the offer and

receive these kingdoms.

- No nation will be free from the reign of the Antichrist, but the focus of the Antichrist will be the destruction of the Jewish people (who by nature of their faith will not worship the beast nor the dragon).

- Note that "the saints" is the Jewish nation of believers, not "anyone who is a Christian."
  - Note also that the Antichrist will *overcome them.*
  - That is, those who are not in the shelter of the Most High (see note on Revelation 12:17 concerning "the remnant of her seed.")

▶ Two groups - verse 8

- All those whose names are written refuse to worship, the rest ("all" of them) will worship the beast and be cast into the lake of fire (Rev. 19:20).

▶ The Hour of Decision - verses 9-10

- Verse 9, the last warning to take heed. After this, it is too late.
- Verse 10 also seems to confirm that the "hour of decision" has passed, and now what is decreed will take place.
- Verse 10 contains a prophetic condemnation of those who serve with the Antichrist, doing his bidding. In short, they will drink their own medicine.
- The saints (believing Israel) can rest assured that "vengeance is mine, saith the Lord."

Revelation 13:11: *The Second Beast*

- **Another beast** - This is the Greek ἄλλος (*allos*), "another of the same kind," rather than *heteros*, "another of a different kind."

- The first beast (the Antichrist) came **out of the sea,** the second **out of the earth**.

  - Since the Greek word for earth (γῆ - *ge*) means either *earth* or *land*, an interpretive decision must be made.
  - It is possible that this beast comes up *out of Israel*. The first beast comes from the Assyrian region of the Greek empire, thus the second could be from the land of Israel.
  - The use of the same word in verse 12 makes *earth* more reasonable, though not essential.

- **He had two horns** -

  - As with the first beast, all pronouns in this chapter are third person neuter to match "beast," not masculine. However, translators have interpreted them in the masculine due to the characteristics of personhood in each.
  - The meaning of the two horns is not as clear as the 10 of the first beast. However, two is typically the number of *witness* or *testimony* in the Bible, and this beast comes to give *witness* to the first beast.
    - This beast appears to be the religious-like prophet of the political beast. His speech is "dragon-like," indicating its source.
    - This beast completes the "unholy trinity" of the Anti-God, Anti-Christ, and Anti-Spirit.

Revelation 13:12-18: *The Work of the Second Beast*

- **He exerciseth all the power -**
  - The Greek word ἐξουσια (*exousia*) is *ek* (out of) *ousia* (substance, wealth, possessions).
  - We get our English word essence from *ousia*.
  - The root is used in Luke 15:12-13 to speak of the goods and substance of the father, given to the prodigal son.
  - The word *exousia* denotes that the power is drawn from the essence or substance that is not inherent. Therefore, this is a word of administrative authority not having power within itself.

- **He causeth -** The following verses list six things that this false prophet causes.
  - Worship of the first beast (v. 12)
  - Fire to come down (v. 13)
  - Creation of a beastly idol (v. 14)
  - Providing life to this idol (v. 15)
  - Killing those who do not worship the idol (v. 15)
  - Instituting the mark of the beast (v. 16)

- **To worship the beast -**
  - The beast is the revived Roman empire and especially it's "Caesar."
  - To understand the danger of "state worship," look to Hitler's Germany or Mao's China.

- **Great wonders -**
  - Christians need to be totally unimpressed with miracles.
  - The Bible is filled with pagans who performed miracles (the wonder-workers of Egypt, Jannes and Jambres, Simon the Sorcerer, etc.).
  - Even the miracles of Jesus meant nothing in and of themselves, but they were "signs," not direct evidence of the Messianic identity of Jesus. They only had authority because they were fulfillments of specific prophecies. See Matthew 11:1-5 for proof.
  - Christians today should reject the "Power Evangelism" approach that calls for miracles as proof of the gospel.
- **He deceiveth -**
  - The Greek πλανος (*planos*) is the root of our English word planets, because the planets «wander» through space. The root is to wander or rove.
  - Without an anchor, the people of the earth will rove, until they find something of essence (the root word of power in v. 12.)
- **That they should make an image to the beast -**
  - The sentence structure here is important. The second beast (subject) deceives (verb) those who dwell on the earth (indirect object) to make (direct object).
  - The people are deceived to make an image. This is confirmed in Revelation 19:20.
  - Rather than one single image, it seems that each person was to make their own individual idol.
  - Notice that a faithful Jew would refuse such a command, therefore there will be a large number of Jews (those who are not in the secret place of the Almighty) who will be killed.

- The power to give life, and to kill (v. 15)
  - It appears that each of the idols will be given breath and ability to report those who do not worship the beast, so that they may be punished with death.
- The giving of a mark (v. 16-17)
  - This sheds light on the statement of Jesus in Matthew 19:23-24 about the challenge for a rich man to enter the Kingdom. In order to maintain their wealth, they will be forced into receiving the mark of the beast...and nobody with this mark will enter the Kingdom.

Revelation 13:18: *The Mark of the Beast*

- The command to count indicates that the mark will be calculable.
  - The same word is used (in the present tense) in Luke 14:28.
  - Here it is used in the aorist tense, giving indication that a person cannot calculate the meaning *today*, but at a point in time *in the future* it will be possible.
- The number of a man - Literally, the Greek says *the number of man*. The beast will identify himself as the "ultimate man" in such a way that it will be calculable.

Revelation 14:1-20: *Looking Ahead*

Revelation 14:1-5: *The 144,000 in the Kingdom*

- Verse 1
  - "Lo!" - This is the common "Behold" imperative of the book of Revelation.

- The Lamb on Mt. Zion - This is the interpretive remark that allows us to know that what follows is a parenthetical statement, a "flash-forward" to the future, when the Lamb, Jesus Christ, shall stand on this earth in Jerusalem, and his throne (v. 3) will be established. Thus, verses 1-5 take place *after* the Second Coming.

▶ Verse 2

- Used three times in verse 2, **Voice** is φωνή [*phone*], which is literally the «sound,» not necessarily a human voice, though it can be.
- This is not the voice of the Lamb, though his voice is as the **voice of many waters** in Revelation 1:15. In Revelation 19:6, the same sound is heard, and is clearly not Christ.
- In Revelation 6:1, the **voice of a great thunder** is one of the four living creatures. In Revelation 19:6, there is also the voice of great thunder.
- This appears to be the same unidentified celebratory sounds/voices as in Revelation 19:6.
- **The voice of harpers harping** - This is either a second **voice** that John hears, or more likely the identification of the **voice of many waters.** The grammatical structure appears to make this a clarification of the first voice.

▶ Verse 3

- The 144,000 is the subject of this verb **sung**.
    - Note that *The Message* has the wrong subject.
    - The **voice from heaven** and the **voice of harpers** in verse 2 appear to be accompaniment and/or harmony, not the singers.
- The verb "to sing" is in the present, so "they sing" would be better

Greek than **they sung** (which is a past participle, equivalent to "they were singing"). Many English translations put this in past tense to align with English grammatical standards.

- How they sing - **as it were a new song**
    - The "as it were" is adverbial, describing the manner of singing--They were singing in the manner that they would sing a new song.
    - In context, it is hard to determine whether this means "their lack of practice showed through" or "they sang with excitement of something new." Either possibility is true.
    - Notice that in Revelation 5:9 the creatures and 24 elders sang a new song, without the adverbial issues.
- Where they sing -
    - **Before the throne** is also adverbial, describing the location of the singing. This is the throne of the Lamb on earth (v. 1).
    - Since this is before the throne of the Lamb, the **four creatures** and the **twenty-four elders** have come to earth.

▶ Verses 4-5 - The description of the 144,000

- All of the descriptors and the grammatical genders used in the verse are masculine, thus the 144,000 must be exclusively male.
- The 144,000 are the **firstfruits**
    - There are several firstfruits in the New Testament.
        - Christ is the firstfruits of them that slept (1 Cor. 15:20,23).
        - Men who were firstfruits of evangelism in various provinces (Rom. 16:5; 1 Cor. 16:15)
        - Jewish believers were a kind of firstfruits of his creatures (Jas. 1:18)

- The 144,000 were the firstfruits unto God and to the Lamb.

These are men who have perfectly obeyed the Mosaic Law and all its commands (v. 5).

Revelation 14:6-7: *The Proclamation of the Everlasting Gospel*

- The Angel - **in the midst of heaven** - Literally, "at the highest point in the sky" i.e.: the zenith.

- The Gospel - A matter of utmost importance is to distinguish the Gospels. Many modern Christians assume there is one Gospel that has always been proclaimed. Scofield mentions the following gospels:

  - The Gospel of the Kingdom - God will establish the earthly reign of His Son, the Messiah. This gospel was proclaimed in the past and will be again proclaimed in the Tribulation.

  - The Gospel of the grace of God - The good news that the penalty has been paid in full by the death, burial, and resurrection, and that eternal life can be received as a grace gift to all who believe.

  - The Gospel of Paul ("my Gospel") - Includes the Gospel of grace but also the fact that those who receive it become "one new man," the body of Christ (the church).

  - The Everlasting Gospel - The message which is to be proclaimed at the arrival of the Messiah. It is good news to those who have endured to the end of the Tribulation.

- The **everlasting gospel** is not one that is to be proclaimed today, but is Everlasting in that, when it is initiated, it is the final Gospel proclamation that lasts for all time.

- The content of the **everlasting gospel-**
  - **Fear God, and give him glory** - This is an imperative. Literally, "be afraid of God."
  - The gospel of fear and worship has been proclaimed in our world, with disastrous consequences. In our dispensation, fear and worship should be *results* of receiving a gift of grace.

Revelation 14:8: *The Proclamation of the Fall of Babylon*

- Like the judgment of verse 7, this verse is a "flash-forward" to the fall of Babylon, which will take place just prior to the judgment.

Revelation 14:9-11: *The Proclamation of the Doom of the Followers of Antichrist*

- Verses 9-11 need no interpretation: all those who will receive the mark of the beast will be cast into the lake of fire.

Revelation 14:12-13: *The Patience of the Saints*

- This is an age in which the remnant of Israel will both **keep the commandments** of the Law and **have the faith of Jesus**. The physical results for many are seen in verse 13.
- Those who refuse the mark are likely going to die. Verse 13 proclaims the blessedness of their death. Note that **their works do follow them** because they will be living in an age of the Law.

Revelation 14:14: *The Victorious Son of Man*

- The **Son of Man** - This is the last use of the phrase in the Bible. It is a Messianic term that denotes the earthly rights and reign of the Messiah. The first use of the term in the New Testament is Matthew 8:20, which contains a complete contrast.

- A **golden crown** - This is the στέφανος [*stephanos*] not *diadem*. That is, the victor's crown, not the crown of the reigning monarch. He will wear the *diadem* in Revelation 19.

- A **sharp sickle** - the word δρέπανον [*drepanon*] comes from *drepo*, which is the word "to pluck." It is a tool used exclusively for harvesting.

Revelation 14:15-16: *The Harvest of the Earth*

- **Another angel** - This is the 4th of a series of seven angels.
  - Verses 6-7, first angel
  - Verse 8, second angel
  - Verses 9-13, third angel
  - Verses 15-16, fourth angel
  - Verse 17, fifth angel
  - Verses 18-20, sixth angel
  - Revelation 15:1, seventh angel

- The instruction: **thrust in...and reap**
  - The final judgment is often referred to as a harvest time.
  - See Joel 3:13-14-15 for more insight.

- The instruction was given to **he that sat on the cloud**.
  - This is the Son of Man, who was the sower and now the reaper.
  - See John 5:27

- Since **the earth was reaped**, this must include both Jews and gentiles.

Revelation 14:17-20: *The Vine into the Winepress of Wrath*

- The fifth angel (v. 17) works in conjunction with the sixth angel (v. 18). This fifth angel harvests the **vine of the earth** (v. 18).
  - There is no definitive interpretation of the **vine of the earth.**
  - The "vine of the earth" is compared to the "vine of God," thus the vine of Antichrist vs. the vine of Christ.
- Verses 18-19 appear to be a foreshadow of the Battle of Armageddon, in which the nations of the earth are gathered together outside Jerusalem.
- The **winepress was trodden without the city** - This speaks of the protection and future use of the city of Jerusalem.

Revelation 15:1-4: *The Great and Marvelous Sign*

- Verse 1
  - The sign was great and **marvelous** - θαυμαστός [*thaumastos*] is of the same Greek word as the English word *theater*, where a person gazes upon a scene.
  - Plagues -
    - The root word is πλησσω [*plasso*], which is "mold-able," from which we get *plastic*.
    - It comes with the meaning of striking an object to mold it.
    - In the Bible, plagues are seen as something used of God to shape society.
  - Why are the plagues last?
    - In Greek, "last" is tied to "because," not "plagues."

- These seven plagues are last because the wrath of God is completed in them.
  - The plagues fill up the wrath of God - **filled up**, or "completed." This is a completion of the "covenant of marvels" of Exodus 34:10.

▶ Verse 2

- **A sea of glass** -
  - Compare to Jeremiah 52:20 where there was a "sea" of "brass." The word sea could be used to speak of the laver before the entrance of the Temple.
  - Whether this is a literal sea or figurative, it gives imagery of the victory of the overcomers.
- **Them that had gotten the victory over the beast… -**
  - This is a present active participle. Literally, "the [people] getting victory." It is not passive ("the people given the victory").
  - Note that under the seals there was a multitude of the redeemed (Rev. 7:9), under the trumpets were the prayers of the saints (Rev. 8:1), and now under the plagues there is a multitude of overcomers.
  - Because these who have gotten victory are in heaven, they are presumably the "remnant of the seed" (Rev. 12:17) who die because they will not take the mark of the beast.
  - The Critical Text does not include **over his mark**. The *Textus Receptus* literally says, *and of its mark of the number of its name*.
  - Note that the Greek references to the Beast are always "it" not "he."

- The overcomers **stand on the sea of glass** -
  - Compare Revelation 2:7, 11, 17, 26, 3:5, 12, 21.
  - These passages, in the light of chapter 15, give evidence to the interpretation of the seven assemblies as future, post-tribulation Jewish assemblies rather than church-age assemblies.
- **Harps of God** - The word κιθάρας [*kitharas*] is the root of the English words *zither* and *guitar*. In the Bible, it is a stringed instrument, most likely the lyre.

▶ Verses 3-4 -

- The **song of Moses** -
  - The song is Deuteronomy 32:1-44.
  - The song of Exodus 15 is "the song of Moses and of Israel" and is also associated with Miriam.
  - The intro to Deuteronomy 32, given in Deuteronomy 31:19-22, declares Deuteronomy 32 to be the Song of Moses.
  - Take special note of Deuteronomy 31:29 concerning "the latter days."
  - According to Deuteronomy 31:19 this song is going to be a "witness against" Israel, and here we see it used by the faithful remnant against the unfaithful nation.
  - The use of this song provides an example of the Jewish means of interpretation of the books of history, in which history in the Biblical text is prophetic of the future. (For further study, look at the Jewish exegetical method called *pardes*.)
- The **song of the Lamb** - Possibly "worthy is the Lamb," from

Revelation 5, or more likely the words immediately following in verses 3-4.

Revelation 15:5-8: *The Seven Angels Introduced*

- The **temple of the tabernacle** - literally, the ναός [*naos*] is the «dwelling place,» or the Holy of Holies.

- The **seven angels came out of the temple** -
  - The seven angels had entered into the Holy of Holies, and were now coming out from the presence of God.
  - Notice that the plagues come out of the Temple. Those who view Heaven and the things of God as "sugar and spice and everything nice" cannot reconcile this fact.

- Seven **golden vials** - Since the angels already have the seven plagues, and are here given the seven bowls, the plagues and the bowls must not be the same thing.

REVELATION 16:1-21:
THE SEVEN VIALS

Revelation 16:1-11: *The First Five Vials*

- Chapter 16 picks up where Revelation 11:15-19 left off. Chapters 12-15 have been a parenthetical statement.

- Just as the plagues of Egypt were literal, the vials of wrath must be seen as literal also. There is absolutely nothing in the context to merit spiritualization or allegorization of these vials.

- The wrath is given to those who **are worthy** (v. 6), that is, "they deserve it."

- The wrath of God is **true and righteous** (v. 7). This is clearly no longer the dispensation of Grace, in which God is "not imputing their trespasses unto them" (2 Cor. 5:19).

- The fifth vial is poured **upon the seat of the beast** (v. 10). Revelation 2:13 refers to "Satan's throne" as being at Pergamum. Could it be that this becomes the headquarters of the Antichrist?

- The Kingdom of Antichrist will **be full of darkness** (v. 10). Compare Joel 2:1-2, 31 and Mark 13:24-25.

Revelation 16:12-16: *The Sixth Vial*

- Verse 12 - **The great river Euphrates**
  - This does not appear to be symbolic, and thus should be taken literally.
  - The Euphrates stretches from Turkey to the Persian Gulf, acting as a natural barrier to ground travel from Iraq and eastward.
  - The drying up of the Euphrates has tremendous political implications, and is possibly even one of the reasons Babylon revolts against the Antichrist (who is in Turkey / Syria). (This assumes that the Antichrist receives the blame or the brunt of the criticism for the drying of the river).

- Verse 12 - **the kings of the east**
  - Literally, "from the rising of the sun."
  - Who are "the kings of the east?"
    - We typically quickly assume they are Persians, Chinese, etc., which may be true.
    - If so, we wonder…
      - …why an angel is preparing their way
      - …why they are distinguished from the "kings of the earth" in verse 14.
    - When Scripture is allowed to shed light, we see some interesting things—
      - Isaiah 40:3 speaks of a path being prepared
      - Ezekiel 43:2 speaks of the glory of God coming from the east
      - Matthew 24:27 speaks of the Son of Man coming from the east to the west

- Isaiah 41:2 speaks of the Righteous man from the east for the judgment of the nations.
- Isaiah 41:5 also speaks of the Islands and the earth being afraid, which rings harmonious with Revelation 16:20.

▸ Verse 13 - 14— **unclean spirits like frogs**

- The spirits were "unclean like frogs."
- It is interpretive whether the spirits themselves had frog-like appearance.
- **Which go forth** – Grammatically, it is ambiguous but likely the "which" should refer to the spirits, not the miracles. Literally, "they (Spirits of demons doing signs) are to go forth…."
- These spirits gather the **kings of the earth and of the whole world.**
  - That is, not only the Kings and their militaries, but men and women of all walks of life.
  - See Joel 3:9-21 for a comparison, especially noting the call to the weak in verse 10.

▸ Verse 14 - **The battle of that great day of God Almighty**

- This is the more Biblical name of the Battle. We call it the "Battle of Armageddon" because of the gathering place mentioned in verse 16.

▸ Verses 15 - an encouragement

- This word is to the Jewish remnant of that future day.
- The church is told that the Day of the Lord will NOT come as a thief (1 Thess. 5:4), because the church is not in "darkness."

- Compare to Revelation 3:3.
- ▸ Verse 16 - Gathered to Armageddon
  - The "he" is the sixth angel of verse 12.
    - The unclean spirits of verses 13-14 gather the kings and peoples of the earth, then the angel gathers them to Armageddon.
    - Many translations use "they" regardless of the singular verb. They do so with the assumption that the closest noun (spirits) of verse 14 is plural, and assume that there is too much space between the singular "angel" in verse 12. I think this assumption is unmerited and that grammar should prevail. Only one ancient text (the Syriac) has the Greek in the plural.
  - **Armageddon:**
    - That is, the mountain of Megiddo.
    - Megiddo is the most prominent city in the Jezreel Valley, which is often called "The Valley of Armageddon," though never in Scripture.
    - Megiddo is not a natural mountain, but a man-made "Tel."

Revelation 16:17-21: *The Seventh Vial*

- ▸ Verse 17 - **it is done**
  - Chronologically, we are at a changing point from this point forward.
  - The last bowl of wrath has been poured out, the end shall come.
- ▸ Verse 19 - **the great city**

- While most assume Jerusalem is "the great city," the rule of "Scripture interprets Scripture" doesn't allow this.
- The exact Greek term "*η πολις η μεγαλη*" [literally, «the city the great"] is used six times in the book of Revelation, and in the other five is exclusively a reference to Babylon.
- Furthermore, the exact term is used only once in the Septuagint, in Genesis 10:12 of Resen, also a city built by Nimrod.
- Presumably, therefore, the «great city» is Babylon, and it will be divided in three parts by the earthquake of verse 18.

▸ Verse 19 - **great Babylon**

- Remember that Babylon was founded as an attack against God's Word, and was so destructive to God's intent that God started a new dispensation based on what took place at Babel, the original Babylon.
- Now, at the end of the "age of the gentiles," God is going to destroy Babylon forever.
- Linguistic note: Babylon is "the place of Babel" just like "Mageddon" is "the place of Megiddo.
- Chronological note: The destruction of Babylon was foreseen in Revelation 14, and is described in Revelation 17-18.

▸ Verse 20 - the Islands and the mountains

- Compare Zechariah 14:10.
- Note that the Greek does not contain a definite article for "mountains," but shows that **every island fled** and *certain* **mountains were not found.**

REVELATION 17-18:
FUTURE BABYLON DESTROYED

Revelation 17:1-2: *Invitation to View the Judgment*

- Verse 1 - Come see the judgment
  - The **judgment of the whore** is the focus of the coming vision.
  - Verses 1-2 give an introduction to what will be seen, the actual scene begins in verse 3.
  - Note that the angel is going to show a singular **judgment.** This is problematic to those who interpret Revelation 17 and 18 to be two judgments, one of the apostate church and another of the city.
- The recipient of judgment is **the great whore**
  - Who is the **great whore?**
    - The **woman** on the **scarlet colored beast** in verse 3,
    - Defined as **Babylon the Great** in verse 5
    - Shown to be **the great city** in verse 18.

---

* For a good explanation of the literal nature of Babylon in Revelation 17-18, read Future Babylon by Charles Dyer, available from Dispensational Publishing House as well as other retail book outlets.

- To conclude that the woman is anything other than the city of Babylon is difficult at best, and almost certainly unmerited. Why do we need to reinterpret that which the Bible has interpreted?

▶ The woman **that sitteth on many waters**
  - The waters are defined in verse 15 as the peoples and nations of the world.
  - "Sitting upon" is indicative of the support that Babylon has and needs from the nations.
  - The **whore** is "riding the wave" of popular support.
  - Note that Jeremiah 51:13 mentions "many waters" as well, in the context of Babylon. The Jeremiah connection gives further indication that we are talking about literal Babylon.

Revelation 17:3-6: *The Woman*

▶ The physical location of the woman (verse 3)
  - The Greek ἔρημος [*eremos*] is desert or **wilderness**.
    - An *eremite* is a person who dwells in the *eremos*.
    - Our English word *hermit* comes from *eremite*.
  - Note that the location of this whore is in **the wilderness**, which is problematic for those who claim that the Babylon of these chapters is either Rome or the Roman system.
    - *Eremos* is used 50 times in the New Testament, always literally. It is not a word that is used figuratively in Revelation or other books of the Bible.
    - The wilderness is the same place the woman who is Israel fled to in Revelation 12:6 and 14.

- The political location of the woman (verse 3)
  - Since the **whore** of verse 1 **sitteth upon many waters** and the **woman** of v. 3 **sit upon a scarlet colored beast**, are they the same woman?
  - Verse 15 appears to confirm the woman and the whore as the same.
  - Just as in verse 1, the act of sitting conveys the support given by the nations and the beast. Babylon would not exist without either.
- The description of the beast -
  - Because this is the same description of the Antichrist in Revelation 13:1, and because the **beast** is the term used exclusively for the Antichrist in Revelation, the identity of the **scarlet colored beast** is unquestionable.
  - The seven heads likely represent the seven empires that attempted to annihilate the Jewish people: Egypt, Syria, Assyria, Babylon, Persia, Greece, and Rome.
  - The ten horns are the 10 last-days Kings of the Roman Empire.
- The golden cup (v. 4) - Compare Jeremiah 51:7
- The name on her forehead (v. 5) -
  - It is without merit that **mystery Babylon** is disconnected with physical Babylon.
  - Beginning in verse 7, the angel reveals all **the mystery of the woman** and declares her to be **the great city** in verse 17.
  - The interpretation of **mystery Babylon** as the apostate church or the Roman Catholic church is built upon these two words alone (without context), followed by *eisegesis*.

- Furthermore, neither the city of Rome nor the Papal system are **the mother of harlots and abominations of the earth.** In fact, both are more the recipient than the originator.

▶ Who is the **mother of harlots** (v. 5)?

- Babylon has been the center of humanism since its creation by Nimrod.
- Humanism is expressed in power, sensuality, greed, and egotism, which are aspects of Babylon from the beginning through the end.

▶ The brutality of the woman toward faith (v. 6) -

- The last days will not only see a rebuilding of Babylon, but a renewed fervor of antisemitism.
- Humanism is always secular, and secularism is always threatened by Judaism and Christianity.
- **Saints** refers to redeemed Israel.
- Who are the **martyrs of Jesus?** The could be an emphasis by repetition, but it is more likely that the **saints** and the **martyrs of Jesus** are two different groups of people. Both are martyrs, but one of the Jewish race and another gentile.

Revelation 17:7-8: *The Angelic Explanation*

▶ Verse 7 - **Wherefore didst thou marvel?**

- What is seen is clearly not in John's expectations.
- Whether this is because Babylon was largely uninhabited in John's day, or a safe-haven for Jews, it is uncertain.

- There is certainly some **mystery** that John does not understand.
- Verse 8 - **The beast that thou sawest…**
  - Whether this is a reference to a death and resurrection of the Antichrist or is (as in Rev. 13:1) a reference to the nations that are contained in the Antichrist system is yet to be seen.
- Names written **from the foundation of the world-**
  - If this is an argument for election, it can only be true for election in the future age of the Tribulation.
  - Since 144,000 are certainly elect for a certain role, it could be reference to them.

Revelation 17: 9-15: *A Further Explanation*

- The mystery explained-
  - John is about to take away the mystery of this scene, but he warns that it is not easy to understand, thus it is for the **mind which hath wisdom.**
- The **seven heads** and the **seven mountains** explained -
  - We have seen the woman sitting on **many waters** (v. 1) as well as upon **a scarlet colored beast** (v. 3).
  - Both times, the **woman** was figurative of Babylon, and that which she sat on was symbolic of something literal. That is, the woman did not literally sit on **many waters** nor upon a **scarlet colored beast**.
  - Rather, she gained her support from the peoples of the earth and from the Antichrist.
  - Now we are told that the woman sits on **seven mountains** which are **seven heads.**

- It is not consistent to take the **mountains** as literal unless we take the **sea** and the **beast** as literal.
- Notwithstanding, most commentaries immediately look for a city with seven mountains (of which there are many: Istanbul (Constantinople), Brussels, Jerusalem, and Rome to start the list).
- Since the **seven heads** and the **seven mountains** must be the same thing, it is without merit whatsoever to understand the **mountains** to be literal.
- Rather, **mountain** is a further description of the **heads**.
- This "mountainification of a person" is not foreign to Scripture - see Jeremiah 51:25 and Zechariah 4:7 and Daniel 2:35.

▶ Verse 10 - the **seven kings** -

- More accurately, "they are." That is, the seven mountains are representative of seven kings.
- This would be much clearer if verse 10 was part of verse 9.
- Note that the heads = mountains = kings, and the heads do not equal kingdoms.
  - This invalidates a previous interpretation that the seven heads were the seven nations that attempted to overthrow the nation of Israel.
  - We must take Scripture at face value and say these seven heads are seven kings.
- Five are fallen:
  - This is at the time of the future vision, not at John's time, nor ours.
  - Therefore, to associate the first six Kings with John's experience in the first century and prior is irresponsible.

- o If we divide the time after the rapture into the *suntelia* (beginning of the end) and *telios* (end), using the words of Matthew 24, then we can say that the Antichrist Beast is, in a manner of speaking, a system of Kings, though one King will be "the Antichrist."
- o In the *suntelia* (prior to the seven years) there will be six kings, one of whom is reigning at the time of this vision.
- o Then the seventh begins and will reign for seven years, which is **a short time**.

▶ Verse 11 - The Beast

- The Beast himself (the Antichrist) is **the eighth** King, who is **of the seven**.
- Perhaps this means that the Antichrist is the seventh of these future kings, and, due to his resurrection, has both a pre- and post fatal wound personality, thus is counted as the seventh and the eighth.

▶ Verse 12 - The 10 Horns

- Since the 10 kings here have not yet received a kingdom, IF these kings are the same as in Daniel's prophecies, then there is no reason for us to look for a ten-nation confederation until late into the Tribulation.
- One hour with the beast - More literally, "the same hour," therefore either the 7 years of the tribulation or the 3 1/2 years of the second half of the tribulation.

▶ Verse 14 - the war with the Lamb

- This 10-King coalition is the coalition of Kings, under the leadership of the Antichrist, that engage in the Battle of Armageddon.

- Verse 15 - the faithful with the Lamb:
  - A Greek word ending in *-os* makes a noun into an adjective.
  - The *pistos (faithful)* are those of *pisteou (faith)*.
  - This therefore does not speak of works, but rather (and more simply) the fact that these are people who can be described as having faith.

Revelation 17:16-18: *A final Explanation*

- Verse 16 - the ten horns
  - It is important to recognize that the 10 Kings are not part of Babylon, but are haters of Babylon and instruments of her destruction.
  - Since the 10 Kings are of the Roman system, it makes it very hard to say "Mystery" Babylon is also of the Roman system. The Kings do not destroy themselves, they destroy Babylon.
- Verse 17 - The godless doing God's work. Even godless men can be used to accomplish God's will!
- Verse 18 - Clarity of the woman:
  - This is the most clear definition that could be given, and there is no merit to disregard the interpretation of Scripture.
  - The woman is a city, not a system, religion, spirit, individual or corporation.
    - Since the woman is a city and the city is real, we should take the name of the city also as real and not a symbol, i.e.: Babylon is the city of Babylon.

Revelation 18:1-3: *The Illuminating Angel*

- Verse 1 - The description of the angel.
  - While we know very little about angels, we can see that they have differing levels of authority and glory.
  - Never before have we seen an angel that illumines the earth with his glory.
- Verse 2 - The forewarning: **Babylon has fallen**
  - This ultimate destruction of Babylon is prophesied by several Old Testament passages, including Isaiah 12-14, 34, Jeremiah 50-51, Zephaniah 2.
  - The Old Testament descriptions of the destruction of Babylon are only consistent with Revelation 17-18, not with any events in history.
- Verse 3 - Summary of the **nations, kings,** and **merchants**
  - The problem of the nations is, literally, "all nations have drunk of her fornication, and thus the wine of the fury of her fornication."
  - The problem is the drinking of her fornication, now the nations are receiving the wrath of that drink.

Revelation 18:4-7: *Instructions for the Jews*

- Verse 4 - There were two announcements given.
  - The first pre-announced the fall of Babylon
  - The second warns **"my people"** to get out of Babylon.
    - **My people** are the Jewish people, some of whom will

doubtless live in Babylon at the time.

- There is a two-fold reason that they should **come out:** for holy living and to avoid her destruction.

▸ Verse 5 - There are two reasons given for the destruction of Babylon.

- Her sins have reached to Heaven
  - On several occasions, the sins of a nation reach a point of no return. Compare Jeremiah 51:9 (Babylon), Genesis 18:20-21 (Sodom & Gomorrah), Jonah 1:2 (Nineveh).
- God has **remembered her iniquities**. (Galatians 6:7 reminds us that **God is not mocked.**)

▸ Verse 6 - 7 - The second instruction for the Jews

- **Reward her** - This imperative is the second person plural, thus an instruction for the Jewish people.
- The word ἀποδίδωμι [*apodidomai*] means to «pay back.»
  - Since Romans 12:17 instructs believers in the age of grace to **recompense no man evil for evil**, using the same Greek word as **reward** in Revelation 18:6, those without a dispensational theology must make up something to explain the "discrepancy."
- **Torment and sorrow give her** - Verse 7 -
  - Also, an imperative to the Jewish people.

Revelation 18:8-19: *The Mourning of the Masses*

▸ Verse 8 - Why give her torment and sorrow?
- On account of the self-glorification of verse 7, the plagues of death, mourning, and famine will come, all very suddenly.

- "Pride goeth before destruction, and a haughty spirit before the fall." (Prov. 16:8)

▸ Verses 9-10 - The mourning of the kings

- The kings of the earth were participants with her, but were not "her."
- This is a further reminder that Babylon is a specific entity, not a system of religion, politics, or economics.
- The kings should be standing in fear because their torment is soon to come.

▸ Verses 11-16 - The mourning of the merchants

- The main reason for their mourning: **for no man buyeth their merchandise any more** (v. 11)
- The list of verse 12: These are things that cannot be spiritualized.
  - This is simply an inventory list of some of the merchandise of the future city.
  - This shows a future prosperous economy centered in Babylon.
  - Beware of those who use the fear of economic collapse to encourage you to give, squander, or horde your wealth in gold coins. Such fear-mongering is largely without basis, Biblical or otherwise.
- The adornment of verse 16: Often commentators will say that Revelation 17 is false religion but Revelation 18 is a false economy. Often, they will take the clothing of the woman in chapter 17 to "prove" that the Roman Catholic religion is the "whore." However, the same woman is in Chapter 18, with the same clothing.

- Verses 17-19 - The mourning of the sailors

    - Why shipmasters in Babylon? Babylon sits on the Euphrates river.

Revelation 18:20-24: *Heaven Rejoices*

- Verse 20 - **God hath avenged her**

    - Literally, "God judged your judgment upon her" --and was in agreement. Thus, God **hath avenged you on her**.

- Verse 21 - The Greek uses the double negative, which is a means of double emphasis in Greek. Literally, "Babylon the great absolutely not at all will be found."

- Verse 24 - From Genesis 11, murder and martyrdom had roots in the Babylonian system that celebrates secular humanism rather than worship of the one true God.

REVELATION 19-20:
THE KING AND HIS KINGDOM

Revelation 19:1-5: *Heaven Rejoices*

- Verse 1
  - The **voice of much people** comes forth, fulfilling the instruction of Revelation 18:20.
  - **Alleluia** is the Greek transliteration of Hallelujah. In the KJV Old Testament, the Hebrew is translated "Praise ye the Lord" (as in Ps. 104:35, which is remarkably corresponding in context). In the New Testament, KJV transliterates as "alleluia."
- Verse 2 - God **hath judged the great whore**.
  - This makes clear that God was "behind the scenes" working through the beast and his 10 kings.
- Verse 3
  - **Again** is the Greek word δεύτερον [*deuteron*] from which we get «Deuteronomy,» which is a repetition of the Law.
  - The smoke of Babylon:
    - In Revelation 18:21, we see that Babylon **shall be found no more at all,** yet here we see her smoke **for ever and ever**.

- This is not a contradiction, since the smoke of her ruins is not the city of Babylon.
- Even in the Millennium, her smoke will remain as a reminder of Babylon and the sin of humanism, for which she was the icon.

▶ Verse 4 - The 24 Elders and the 4 Living Creatures

- What a picture of rejoicing as the 24 elders and 4 living creatures rejoice in the finality of the judgment.

▶ Verse 5

- **Praise our God, all ye his servants,** is a quote of Psalm 135:1, which must be used to identify the **servants**. In the context of Psalm 135, this is a reference to Israel's faithful.
- **Ye that fear him, both small and great** is a quote of Psalm 115:13, which is described as "the house of Israel" in Psalm 115:12.
- The two Psalms quotes of Revelation 19:5 are a fulfillment of the promised blessing of Matthew 5:10-12.

Revelation 19:6-10: *The Lamb, His Bride, and the Marriage Feast*

▶ Verse 6

- Because Greek doesn't have a "time" sense, as in English, this *aorist* tense for **reigneth** must be interpreted.
- The aorist is often translated in past tense, but past is not inherent in the aorist.

- Rather, aorist is used for something that takes place at a particular point in time, whether past, present, or future.
- NKJV, NASB, ESV, NIV and many others say "reigns," which implies a *perfect* tense which is not in the Greek.
- My own interpretation is that this is a foreshadow of the almost-arrived reign, therefore is future. See note of verse 7 for confirmation on this interpretation.

▶ Verse 7 - **Be glad and rejoice, and give honour**

- The three verbs are in the subjunctive, which is the tense of potentiality.
- The verbs **Be glad** and **rejoice** are only used in the subjunctive in this verse and nowhere else in the New Testament.
- The verb **give honour** is used in the subjunctive in six other places in the New Testament (Mk. 6:37, 12:15 [twice]; Jn. 1:22; 1 Cor. 9:12; 2 Thess. 3:9).
    - Each of those six times, the KJV translates the verb as future.
    - This is evidence that the aorist of verse 7 is a future aorist, not present or past.

▶ Verse 7 - **the marriage of the Lamb**

- While the church has read herself into the position of the Lamb's bride, the Scripture never states such to be the case, and gives plenty of evidence otherwise.
- There are numerous references to the Kingdom of God as a wedding feast (Matt. 22:2, 25:1, etc.).
- Revelation 22 identifies the bride.
- Further, the church does not "make herself ready," but is made ready by grace through faith.

- The church has nowhere been in the context of this chapter, but the **servants** (Israel) have been in the context.
- While we read the church into verse 9, we should rather read Scripture and let it interpret itself.
- Compare, for example, Isaiah 54:1-5, which speaks of the land of Israel as the bride. To read ourselves into the bride's position is nothing but arrogance.

▸ Verse 8 - **the righteousness of saints**
  - These words serve as further evidence that the church is NOT the bride.
  - For the church, Christ is our righteousness (1 Cor. 1:30).
  - For the **saints** (Jewish believers in the Kingdom age), they **overcome** and their works of the Law and their belief in the Messiah are their righteousness.
  - Without this perspective, many passages in Revelation become contradictory with the grace passages of Paul.
  - Compare this with Matthew 22, which speaks of the Marriage feast with many guests, yet some of the guests do not have the proper garments. Such a parable doesn't fit with the age of grace, but does fit in the Kingdom age.
  - The Greek word translated **righteousness** in KJV is δικαιώματα [*dikaiomata*].
    - Greek words ending in -*ma* or -*mata* mean "the result or visible outcome" of the root word.
    - In English, we have *stigmata, schemata, ultimate*.
    - If God had wanted to talk about the **righteousness** rather than the **righteous acts**, He would have used the word δικαιοσύνη [*dikaiosyne*].

- This is one reason I am a KJV proponent, but not an adherent to KJV only.

▸ Verse 9 - **they which are called**

- The bride is not a guest at her own wedding, nor does she receive an invitation. So those who are called to the marriage supper are both the Jewish people (who rejected the call) and those in the "highways and byways" (compare Matt. 22). The "chosen" of Matthew 22 is the Jewish remnant of the last days. Note that the supper took place before the marriage.

▸ Verse 10

- Since the angel is talking to John, one could assume that **thy bretheren that have the testimony of Jesus** are Jewish believers.
- To **have the testimony** is to have both heard it and taken hold of it. Compare Revelation 12:17.
  - The word **prophecy** has a definite article, so literally "the prophecy," that is, "the prophecy" of the book of Revelation (as in Rev. 22:18-19). From Revelation 1:1 we were told that this prophecy is **the revelation of Jesus Christ.**

Revelation 19:11-16: *The Second Coming Seen*

▸ Verse 11

- Those who teach the book of Revelation symbolically almost never take this symbolically.
- It is notable that the two things mentioned of the returning Savior are His judgment and His warfare. The age of grace will have ended, and judgment will have come.

- Verse 12
  - If no one knows the name but **he himself**, it would be useless to speculate what that name is.
- Verse 13
  - A robe dipped in blood: Compare Isaiah 63:1-3.
  - His name is called the **Word of God**. A very clear reference to John 1:1.
    - It does not seem that this is the name referred to in verse 12, since Christ as the **Word of God** was known in John's Gospel.
- Verse 14
  - Who are these armies?
    - Many say that these are the saved people from the rapture, and it could be, but the answer is not given.
    - The closest Biblical interpretation would be to take the 200 million-strong army of the four angels at the Euphrates (Rev. 9:14-16) as this same army. This interpretation requires
      - A rejection of any kind of Chinese or Indian interpretation of Revelation 9:14-16
      - Seeing the angels of Revelation 9:14-16 as "good" angels rather than demonic
      - Rejecting the interpretation of the raptured church as the army.
  - Why has the common interpretation been that this is the church?

- We like to read ourselves into as many Scriptures as possible.
- The robes of **fine linen, white and clean** are considered to be the church because of the reference to similar linens in the Bride of Christ and in the church at Sardis (Rev. 3:2).
- Since both of these are often interpreted as describing the church, it is presumed that this passage must also be about the church.
  - An important principle of interpretation: don't make the Bible say more than it says.
    - All we can conclude is that he is accompanied by an army.
    - We could surmise that this is the army of Revelation 9:14-16, or we could speculate that it is the raptured church.

▸ Verse 15

  - The word **rule** is from ποιμην [*poimen*] which is often translated "shepherd."
  - Remember this when you say, "Our pastor doesn't have good shepherding skills."

▸ Verse 16

  - This gives a definitive identity of the One on the horse. Revelation 17:14 identifies the King of kings and Lord of lords as **the Lamb.**
  - NOTE: the capitalization is a style matter selected by the interpreters.

Revelation 19:17-19: *The Battle of Armageddon*

- These verses give the chronology of the Battle of Armageddon, described in Revelation 16.

- Note that while many take the army in verse 14 to be the raptured church, they don't apply this so vividly by verse 19.

Revelation 19:20-21: *The Outcome of the Battle*

- Verse 20

    - Grammatically, this is one group of people. Why were these people deceived? Because of the **strong delusion, that they should believe a lie** that God sends (2 Thess. 2:11).

    - This is the first time we see the lake of fire. Assuming that this is chronologically correct, the Antichrist (Beast) and the False Prophet are the first to enter the lake of fire, even before Satan, who does not enter until after the 1,000 years (Rev. 21:10).

- Verse 21

    - If this **remnant** is **them that had received the mark of the beast, and them that worshipped his image** (v. 20), then we can conclude that:
        - Nobody with the mark of the beast will enter heaven
        - The Kingdom of God (millennium) begins only with "overcomers" who endured the tribulation without succumbing to the delusion of the Beast.

    - Note that some teach that repentance is possible after receiving the mark of the beast.

- For example, Phil Johnson of Grace to You, "Revelation 19:20 indicates that multitudes will take the mark of the Beast because they are deceived. Scripture does not say that they are thereby automatically hardened forever against repentance." (https://www.gty.org/blog/B131030).
- This "potential forgiveness" position assumes that…
  - The Age of Grace is continuing during this future time
  - The delusion can be overcome once accepted.

Revelation 20:1-3: *The Binding of Satan*

- Verse 1 – the angel with the key
  - The abyss:
    - Note from Revelation 9:2 - "Bottomless" is *abussos,* which is *a-* (the negator) and *buthos* (a deep pool of water, even the ocean). It is literally, "without depth."
    - The word is often not translated in many English versions, but left as "abyss," as in Luke 8:31 or Romans 10:7 in NASB. It is the home of "the beast" in Revelation 17:8, and the place where Satan is imprisoned by an angel, who is given the key, in Revelation 20:1-3.
    - The abyss is *not* hell, but is a place of imprisonment for demonic forces.
- Verse 2
  - **Laid hold**--This is a power word, based on *kratos*, from which we get all of our ""*cracy" words, such as democracy, theocracy, etc.

- **That old serpent** - This is one of the final chapters in that Genesis 3:15 promise that is the "tent peg" for the plot-line of Scripture.
- **Bound him** - This is the only place in the Bible where Satan is bound. 100% of the charismatic teaching of "binding Satan" is man-made, and is a result of a-millennial or post-millennial Kingdom theology.
- **A thousand years** - This period is the *millennium*, upon which all pre-mil, post-mil, and a-mil theology is built. The Greek word is χίλιοι [*chilioi*] upon which the word *chiliasm* is built. Chiliasm is the word used in church history for millennial beliefs. Prior to Augustine, the belief of a literal 1,000 year Kingdom was very widely taught.

▸ Verse 3

- Shut up and sealed:
    - The Critical Text changes this to "shut *it* and sealed *it*", with the reference being the pit, rather than Satan.
    - Since the emphasis is on the chain that binds Satan, it seems more accurate that Satan was **shut up** and **a seal** was set upon **him**.
    - Whether or not the abyss was shut up and sealed is irrelevant. Furthermore, the shutting and sealing was done so that "**he should deceive the nations no more.**" It is about Satan, not the abyss.
- Satan's deception:
    - The English word *planets* comes from this root word, πλανη [*plane*].
    - The planets were so named because they «wander.» Satan›s

role, from Genesis 3, was to get man to wander around rather than stay put in the Word of God.

- **"till"** –
  - This is always a time word, and therefore is significant to dispensational readers. The word indicates that something is going to fundamentally change in the future.
- **A little season** –
  - Literally a *μικρον κρονον* [*micron kronon*], or «little time.»
  - Since the Greek has ability to speak in general of short times and long times, and since this passage uses the term 1,000 years repeatedly, why would some say that the 1,000 years is just «a long time.»
  - This is unmerited and unmitigated rejection of the meaning of words.

Revelation 20:4-6: *The First Resurrection*

▶ **I saw thrones** –

- Who is "they" that sit upon these thrones and judge?
- Avoid speculation, and allow Scripture to answer the question.
- The most likely possibility is Matthew 19:28: Jesus and His 12 Apostles.
- The 24 Elders also sit on thrones (Rev. 4:4), but no indication is given that they judge the dead.
- 1 Corinthians 6:2 speaks of saints judging the world, but this is a judgment of the dead, so the verse is only mildly relevant.

- **The souls of men** – Though this could be more than one group of people (the beheaded plus those who hadn't received the mark), in its context it is better to read as a collective group of those martyred during the Tribulation.

- **They reigned** - The reign with Christ is also shared by faithful believers - 2 Timothy 2:12.

- **The rest** - This is perfect evidence that the judgment is for the martyrs of the Tribulation, not the "overcomers."

- **The first resurrection** –

  - Remember that John is speaking to a Jewish audience, using Jewish language and theology.
  - Luke 14:14 Jesus spoke of the "resurrection of the just."
  - Since the church and its resurrection was "hidden in God," it makes sense that this is the first resurrection of the Jewish scriptures.

- **The second death** - The second death is the Lake of Fire.

Revelation 20:7-10: *The Satanic Revolt*

- Verse 7 – The thousand years expired

  - Remember the importance of the "'till" in verse 3. This time-word is always important in dispensationalism.
  - Now, in verse 7, the "dispensation of Satan's imprisonment" is complete, and Satan will be loosed for the **little season** prophesied in verse 3.
  - Note that verse 3 says he **must be** released. Why?

- Any answers would be speculation, but it could be that he must be released in order to show his complete rejection of his created purpose (he is beyond rehabilitation) and to give the millennial age inhabitants (who have not been glorified) the same ability of free-will as Adam and Eve.

▶ Verse 8 – **to deceive the nations**

- or "the ethnicities," as in "all the people of the world."
- **Gog and Magog** are most likely given as nations which represent **the four quarters of the earth.**
- Note that this battle is not the same as found in Ezekiel 38-39, which happens before the millennium.
  - Ezekiel 39:25 states that the restoration of Judah will happen after the Ezekiel battle.
  - By this battle in Revelation 20:8, Judah and the 12 tribes have been gathered and living in peace for 1,000 years.

▶ Verse 9 – The circle and the fire

- Even to the end, the Jewish nation and the city of Jerusalem are hated.
  - They are hated because of her chosen status, because she is "the apple of God's eye," and because Jerusalem is the chosen dwelling place of God.
  - Humanism (which is always satanic) cannot allow these to survive.
- Notice that there is no battle, simply the immediately destructive fire from heaven.

▶ Verse 10 – **The lake of fire**

- This is the 2nd arrival into the Lake of Fire. The Beast and False

Prophet were cast in 1,000 years prior.

- Every indication is that all the inhabitants of the Lake of Fire will suffer this torment. The Bible does not teach annihilationism.

Revelation 20:11-15: *The Great White Throne Judgment*

- Verse 11 – The Final Judgment

  - Many Catholic and Reformed traditions have the idea of a "general judgment."
    - Such idea is foreign to Scripture, which teaches two "particular" judgments, in addition to the individual account given by those in the church age.
    - 1 Corinthians 15 speaks about the order of the particular judgments.
  - The destruction of the elements is "the Day of God" seen in 2 Peter 3:10-12.

- Verses 12-13 – the gathering of "the rest of the dead" (see v. 5).

- Verse 14 – the second death

  - Though the KJV translates the Greek ᾅδης [*hades*] as **hell**, hades is actually the place of departed spirits (not bodies).
    - After the resurrection of Jesus Christ, hades was emptied of those who were saved by the blood of Jesus Christ.
    - At one time, hades (sheol in the Old Testament) had a place of paradise and a place of torment.
    - Since the resurrection, it is solely a place of torment.

- The Lake of Fire is the **second death**. The first death is that of the body, whereupon the spirit of the unsaved goes to hades and the spirit of the saved is with the Lord.

▸ Verse 15 – the destination of the unsaved

- Both for the saved and the unsaved there is a judgment of works (2 Cor. 5:10 and Rev. 20:12). However, these are not "salvation" judgments. The ultimate entrance to the New Heaven and New Earth is based on the name being found in the Book of Life.
- All those whose names are not in the Book of Life will spend eternity in the torment of the Lake of Fire.
  - For this reason, we beg others to **be reconciled to God.**

REVELATION 21-22:
THE NEW HEAVEN AND NEW EARTH

Revelation 21:1-5: *The New Revealed*

- Verse 1
  - The new heaven/earth is a necessary conclusion to Revelation 20:11.
  - The new "heaven" could either be the skies (outer space) or literal Heaven.
  - The word new καινὸν [*kainon*] is new in quality, not just time.
  - **No more sea:** There is no reason in the grammar to take this as anything other than literal.
- Verse 2
  - Here, finally, we have the city for which Abraham sought (Heb. 11:10)
  - The fact that Jerusalem is **prepared as a bride** is not enough evidence to claim Jerusalem is the bride. However, other Scriptures confirm her role the bride.
- Verse 3
  - At least since the departure of God's glory from the Temple, the Tabernacle of God has been in Heaven.

- Verse 4
  - An interesting, but unanswered question: will there be any more birth? There will not be pain in childbearing, if there is any childbearing at all.
  - These and following verses are often used to describe Heaven as it exists now. However, they are actually a description of the New Heavens and New Earth. The state of our loved ones who have preceded us in death is not given, other than to be "with the Lord."

Revelation 21:6-8: *A Word to the Wise Living in Tribulation*

- Verse 6
  - Since the earliest days, humanity has been searching for the "fountain of youth," by whatever name. It is a fruitless search. There is no reason to spiritualize the **fountain of the water of life** any more than there is to spiritualize the Tree of Life.
  - Note that "Alpha and Omega" can be either the Father or the Son, but "beginning and end" is always the Father, and "First and Last" is always the Son.
- Verse 7
  - Verses 7-8 are spoken to those living in the days of the coming Tribulation.
  - Like the rest of the book, this is clearly written with people in mind who are not living in the Age of Grace. Without gross spiritualization of words, **overcome** is not a word that is free from personal effort.

- In the Age of Grace, we become children of God by grace through faith.

▸ Verse 8

- This list is given as the opposite of **overcomers** in verse 7.

Revelation 21:9-27: *New Jerusalem Described*

▸ Verse 9

- Note that what John is about to be shown has been seen in a general sense in verse 2. Now it will be shown in more detail.
- Note also that the Lamb's wife (the Bride of Christ) is not the church, unless there is some radical spiritualization of terms.

▸ Verse 12

- Even in the New Jerusalem, the tribes of Israel are eternally commemorated.

▸ Verse 14

- These Apostles are the 11 faithful plus Matthias.
- Paul was a different kind of Apostle, and not an Apostle to the Jews.
- The 12 Apostles have, by the time of the New Jerusalem, been judging Israel for 1,000 years.

▸ Verse 16

- The word *tetragon* is equivalent to our word *quadrangle* - any shape with four sides. The following words of verse 16 describe the city as square.

- **Furlong** is the Greek σταδίων [*stadion*] which was Latinized to *stadium*. A Roman *stadion* was approximately 600 feet. This became the length of a *furrow* and the length of the furrow became the measurement for an *acre*.

▶ Verse 17

- A πηχῶν [*pechon*], which was the measurement from the elbow to the tip of the middle finger.
- **The measure of a man…an angel:** This is a bit unclear, but could be saying that an angelic body is like a human body.

▶ Verse 23

- The sun, moon, and stars had four roles at creation: signs (information), seasons (agriculture), days (rotation), and years (revolution). There is now no further need since all information has been revealed, agriculture is now provided through the tree of life and fountain of life, and time is no more.
- This is a return to days 1-3 of creation, where there was light but no sun. However, in days 1-3 the light source (presumably the glory of God made visible) was from outside the earth, and because of the rotation of the earth there was day and night, even without sun. Now that God is dwelling on earth in the New Jerusalem, the rotation of the earth (if there is rotation) does not cause darkness (see v. 25).

Revelation 22:1-6: *The Things Which Shall Quickly Come to Pass*

▶ Verse 1

- The guide is one of the Angels who had the seven bowls of

wrath, Revelation 21:19.

- River is ποταμος [*potomos*] from which the Potomac River is named.
  - This river is similar to the river from the throne in Ezekiel 47, but since that is a millennial river and this is the New Jerusalem, there are only similarities.
  - There is also similarity with the "old" throne room as seen in Revelation 4:7.
- The river was **clear as crystal.**
  - Bright or Shinning would be a better translation of λαμπω [*lampo*], from which we get the English word *lamp*.

▸ Verse 2

- The πλατυς [*platus*] is literally a «broad place,» and only a street by interpretation.
  - We get the English word *plateau* from this root.
  - It could be the "broad place of the river," with perhaps an island in the middle, or it could be a reference to the street leading to the throne.
- See Revelation 21:16 for the same word used as "breadth."

▸ Verse 3

- With the removal of the curse, the created order is once again, "very good." The Tree of Life is once again available for all of mankind.
- **His servants shall serve him** - This is the closest we have to any indication of what we will do in eternity future.

▸ Verse 4

- His name was previously written on the foreheads of the 144,000.

- In Eternity Future, all who are there will have the safety of the seal of God in the same way the 144,000 did in the Tribulation.

▶ Verse 5

- In Revelation 21:25, we had the revelation that there was no night. This elaboration indicates that there will also not be "shadow," but perpetual light in all locations, meaning the glory of God will be in all locations.

▶ Verse 6

- The word τάχος [*tachos*] is better translated as *quickly*.
- It describes the speed at which the things will come, not the timing of their arrival.

Revelation 22:7-13: *The Coming Reward*

▶ Verse 7

- The word **keepeth** is τηρεω [*tareo*], which is also the root word for our English *theater*. A theater is where you *watch* something.
- The promised blessing is for those who will *watch* (and thus pay attention to) the **prophecy of this book.**
- It is an echo of Revelation 1:3.

▶ Verse 8

- The angel puts himself in the same category as man. This does not mean that men become angels, but that there are really two broad classifications in Eternity Future: God, and God's servants.

- Verses 10-11

  - By necessity **the time** spoken of here must be a reference to the apocalypse of Jesus Christ, the day of the Lord.
  - Verse 11 would be in opposition to both the Great Commission during the age of the Kingdom Offer and 2 Corinthians 5:20 during the age of the church.

- Verse 12

  - This is the last use of the command to **behold**. It has been used 30 times in the book of Revelation.
  - Though this is likely a call to those dwelling in the post-grace dispensation Tribulation age, 1 Corinthians 3:12-14 also states that believers will receive rewards for works.

Revelation 22:14-19: *Final Instructions*

- Verse 14

  - Note again the very problematic issues if this is spoken to the church, since this is a works-based promise.
  - Compare also Revelation 2:7, which shows that the churches are future Jewish assemblies, not current church-age congregations.

- Verse 16

  - The direct application of the book of Revelation is for the Jewish assemblies of the Tribulation era.

- Verse 19

  - By theological necessity, the warning about taking away must be directed to those living after the Age of Grace has concluded.

- In the Age of Grace, salvation is secure and free from the kind of threat that is included in this verse.
- The value of dispensationalism is that it harmonizes the Scriptures.

Revelation 22:20-21: *The Amen!*

▶ Verse 20

- This verse shows the anticipation from Jesus for the future unveiling
- This was His will when He prayed, "Not my will but Thine be done."

▶ Verse 21

- John concludes with GRACE, because he is living in an age of grace.

A NEW LOOK AT THE SEVEN CHURCHES OF REVELATION

Revelation 1:1: *What the Book of Revelation is About*

- Revelation is ἀποκάλυψις [*apokalypsis*], which is an unveiling or revealing.
- What is revealed?
  - NOT the future.
  - Grammatically, it is Jesus Christ who is revealed.
  - This is not a revelation by Jesus but of Jesus. The form of the noun is the same as in the **birth of Jesus** (Matt. 1:18) or the **word of Jesus** (Matt. 26:75) or the **cross of Jesus** (John 19:25).
- The same word (*apokalypsis*) is used in 1 Corinthians 1:7, **waiting for the coming of our Lord Jesus Christ.**
- This **revelation of Jesus Christ** is the subject of the entire book, and it was **signified…by his angel unto his servant John.**
- Question to ponder: if the book of Revelation is about the unveiling of Jesus Christ, why would chapters 2 and 3 be about the church age?

- It is a question which should cause us to have an open mind.
- The answer to the question doesn't solidly confirm anything...yet.

Revelation 1:10: *Where John is When he Writes*

Does this mean that John was in a spiritual ecstatic experience on Sunday? Or that he was "spiritually (not physically) taken to the Lord's day?"

▸ Concerning "in the Spirit" or "in spirit," compare to Matthew 22:43 and John 1:24 for a meaning which simply implies "non-physical."

- Note that there is no definite article (which is often implied in Greek, so may or may not be inserted into the English translation). Either interpretation is possible.
- Note also that KJV is inconsistent when compared to Revelation 4:2, 17:3, and 21:10, which are the only other times the phrase is used in Revelation. The reader should always beware of capitalization for Deity in any English translation.

▸ Concerning "on the Lord's day," most translators (and some translations) make the assumption that this is speaking of Sunday.

- Using the principle of allowing Scripture to interpret itself, this is suspicious.
- There is no reference to Sunday as "the Lord's day," but many references to "the day of the Lord," which is that period of judgment at the end of days.
- It is my belief that this verse tells us that John was spiritually (not physically) taken forward in time to the Day of the Lord, which is given by God to Jesus, and John is going to record what happens, in advance.

Is Revelation 1:19 an Outline of the Book?

I think verse 19 has often been made to say more than it says.

▸ A typical interpretation:

- **the things which thou hast seen** – chapter 1
- **the things which are** – chapters 2-3
- **the things which shall be** – chapters 4-22

▸ Consider verse 2, which says that John wrote "all things that he saw." So, unless John is referring to his previous work of the Gospel of John, then John is telling us that he wrote this introduction (Ch. 1) AFTER he had seen all these things and written about them. Thus, as is commonly done, the intro was written LAST.

- If this is an accurate assumption, then "the things which thou has seen" are words spoken in summary, after John had actually seen something.
- The "things which are" are actually the things revealed in the Revelation.
- Another translation could be "write the things which you've seen, even which are and are to come."
- Or, it could even be "write the things which you have seen, what they are, and are to come."

▸ The question becomes: Is John to write about three things or one thing? Grammatically, it could go either way.

▸ In light of Revelation 1:1, it seems that one thing is in order.

What Happens When You Apply Revelation 2-3 Today?

A Few Problematic Passages

▶ The Church at Ephesus

- Revelation 2:5 - Strange language for the church at Ephesus, whose blessings are "in the heavenlies," especially in light of Romans 11:29. However, if this is a future Jewish assembly, then this makes sense.

- Revelation 2:7 - From a church perspective, this is somewhat problematic. From a futurist perspective, it is perfectly in harmony. See Revelation 21:7.

▶ The Church at Smyrna

- Revelation 2:10 - In a non-futurist presentation the interpreter is left to speculation as to what this refers to. The instruction to be **faithful unto death** fits better with the tribulation period, such as Matthew 10:22.

- Revelation 2:11 - This statement is problematic in a non-futurist interpretation of the letters to the churches.

▶ The church at Thyatira

- Revelation 2:22-23 - This passage is problematic except with a futurist view, since it threatens **great tribulation** on all except those who repent.

- Revelation 2:26 - Under what circumstances does this fit for the Age of Grace? It is only fitting for the Jewish age, prior to the mystery of the church, and after the church's rapture.

- The Church at Sardis

  - Revelation 3:2 – **I have not found thy works perfect** - This is problematic in the age of Grace, in which we are complete in Christ, and our sufficiency is in Christ. Works are a response to grace not a requirement of grace.

  - Revelation 3:4 - Yet another statement that is incompatible with the age of grace, in which our worthiness comes through Christ.

  - Revelation 3:5 - To align this with the age of grace requires verbal gymnastics.

- The Church at Philadelphia

  - Revelation 3:10 - This is a clear reference to the tribulation, and clearly teaches that the protection of God will come because of keeping **the word of my patience**. This is incompatible with the church age which is **delivered...from the wrath to come** by Jesus.

- The Church at Laodicea

  - Revelation 3:16 - If this is written of the church age, can anyone have assurance?

  - Revelation 3:21 - As in the Gospels (before Paul), the right to reign with Christ comes from sacrifice.

Dispensational Publishing House is striving to become the go-to source for Bible-based materials from the dispensational perspective.

Our goal is to provide high-quality doctrinal and worldview resources that make dispensational theology accessible to people at all levels of understanding.

Visit our blog regularly to read informative articles from both known and new writers.

And please let us know how we can better serve you.

Dispensational Publishing House, Inc.
PO Box 3181
Taos, NM 87571

Call us toll free 844-321-4202

www.ingramcontent.com/pod-product-compliance
Lightning Source LLC
Chambersburg PA
CBHW071627080526
44588CB00010B/1297